SOUTH AFRICAN PARALEGALISM
&
HOLISTIC MEDIATION

Johan Claassens (Mpsy.D) Ph.D
written by a Paralegal for Paralegals

MYEBOOK
WE EMPOWER AUTHOR

TITLES BY THE AUTHOR

Africa Calling

The Highly Intuitive Child and Psychological Disorders

Christianity, Spirituality, Satanism and Mental Disorders

South African Paralegalism and Holistic Mediation

I CHOOSE

To live by choice, not by chance

To be motivated, not manipulated,

To be useful, not used,

To make changes, not excuses,

To excel, not compete.

I choose self-esteem, not self-pity,

I choose to listen to my inner voice,

Not to the random opinions of others.

I choose to do the things that you

Won't so I can continue to do

the things you can't.

"Education is the most powerful weapon which you can use to change the world."

– NELSON MANDELA

ACKNOWLEDGEMENTS

Thank you to all the attorneys I have had the privilege of working with and those who I have crossed swords with in various matters. I learned from each and every one of you. You have made my legal journey an interesting one. On this journey I have met some of the sharpest and most knowledgeable minds.

To all the Clerks of Court, I thank you for your patience as I was learning my way around the passages of your courts

To all the magistrates whom I had the pleasure of meeting, your sternness taught me more about law than any law book.

A big thank you to Black Sash for their informative booklet.

Thank you to the team at MYeBook for guiding me through the self-publishing process and for crafting the cover and interior that brought my book to life.

Last but not least a big thank you to my wife who put up with my many hours of research and very slow typing of this book.

"The three A's to ultimate fulfilment:

ACKNOWLEDGE, APPLY, ATTAIN."

– DELLA HARBIN

ABOUT THE AUTHOR

I started my adult life off in business and at a late stage changed direction into psychology and law.

It has indeed been a journey of soul fulfilment and happiness. After completing my Ph.D in Holistic Life Counselling, Mpsy.D in Metaphysical Psychology, I completed my mediator's certification with FAMSA.

Completing my certification in Psycho-Legal fundamentals made me realise that to understand law is to understand people and their behaviours. Human behaviour is in my opinion one of the fundamental foundations of mediation and law.

I studied for my paralegal diploma through the South African School of Paralegal Studies and would highly recommend this institution.

At an age where most people are retiring I am only finding my mojo.

I urge all paralegals to continue studying as our country is changing weekly and before you know it, we as paralegals will be appearing in court on minor matters.

Never in the history of our country has the time been so ready for committed paralegals to grow and "become".

I pray and hope to see the day paralegals are "seen" as an important spoke in a very big wheel. May the time come where each and every paralegal wears their "badge" with pride as they take on the legal world by storm?

May you all be blessed with a mentor that sees your value?

"There is nothing like a dream
to create the future."
– VICTOR HUGO

CONTENTS

PROLOGUE

I do not believe there is any other way of starting this book other than with a Keynote Address speech by the Deputy Minister of Justice and Constitutional Development, the Hon John Jeffery MP at the 1st National Conference on Paralegalism hosted by the Department of Law, Tshwane University of Technology at the ABSA Conference Centre, Montana, Tshwane, 23rd February 2015. I have typed the speech precisely as printed on the justice website. www.justicegov.za

---

Thank you for the kind invitation; it is indeed a pleasure for me to be here at the very first National Conference on Paralegalism. The role played by paralegals in the history of our country is closely linked to our struggle for freedom.

Under apartheid the justice system was repressive, brutal and dehumanising. Legal services and legal advice were generally unavailable to black people. The majority of our country's people had nowhere to go when faced with legal problems. Whilst Legal Aid did exist in theory, in reality it was ineffective and inaccessible. For example, from 1975 – 1976, only 810 applications were approved by Legal Aid for legal aid in criminal cases. If one imagines the large number of criminal cases, were predominately black people, but also others, faced charges under draconian apartheid laws it is clear that legal aid was simply unable to deliver. So where did they go for assistance? They went to paralegals, mostly working in community advice offices, CAO's, as we call them. Paralegals were at the coal-face. They were often the very first port of call for those who had nowhere else to turn.

Jackie Dugard and Katherine Drage, in an article on paralegalism, highlighted the work of the Black Sash. The Black Sash set up paralegals in community advice offices in urban areas to assist black people who contravened the apartheid laws, particularly these that restricted freedom of movement. These offices provided support and free paralegal services, addressing concerns around housing, unemployment pensions, influx control, and detention without trial. Between the 1960's and the 1980's, Black Sash CAO's flourished, and provided evidence with which the group informed its public protests and its monitoring of government policy, legislation, and action, as well as court activities. This allowed the Black Sash to also monitor and record protests, rallies, arrests, detentions and deaths. Today paralegals are still in most cases, the first line of assistance. Many people, in particular people who are poor, marginalised and vulnerable and do not have the resources to access private lawyers, turn to paralegals.

In short, paralegals play many roles. They are often more than paralegals they are also activists, counsellors and educators. A paralegal needs to have knowledge of the law and its procedures, has to know about conflict resolution and must be an activist too, with the commitment, attitude and skill to help people and communities with their legal, human rights, administrative, constitutional and development problems, while at the same time empowering them.

The ambit of a paralegal role is a wide one; a paralegal may investigate and refer matters to lawyers or relevant bodies for them to deal with. They can become educators of the law and rights for people in their communities. They can, play a leading and supportive role in campaigns for improving community living standards and general community development. They fulfil a very important role in the broader justice system. From the side of the government, we value the role of paralegals in the quest for justice for all. Our department, the Department of Justice and Constitutional Development, is pleased to announce that we have recently placed 200 paralegals at our courts, so as to provide capacity on quasi-judicial processes.

Legal Aid SA is one of the biggest employers of paralegals in the country. Their 2014 Annual Report also makes mention of its paralegal capacity. Providing general legal advice is an important part of Legal Aid SA's service delivery programme. This is done through the dedicated paralegal capacity at their 128 offices as well as the national call centre, the Legal Aid SA Advice Line. In the last finance year a total of 328'979 general advice consultations were conducted. This represents a growth of 10% over the previous financial year.

On the issue of the broader justice system and access to justice, let me say that we still have many challenges, the most fundamental being how to enhance access to justice given limited resources. The reality is that many people live in rural areas and not all South African are literate. Even for those who are literate, the law and the legal system are complex, often overwhelming and not always easy to understand. Since 1994 there have been many initiatives and interventions to make justice more accessible. From the side of our Department we have rolled out 330 Small Claim Courts and strengthened the capacity and funding of Legal Aid SA. We have transformed our judiciary, passed many ground-breaking new laws and undertook education and awareness program to inform people of their human rights. We have built new courts, renovated old ones, and brought the courts closer to the people. The construction of new High Courts in Limpopo and Mpumalanga is underway and these courts will be opened as part of the Presidential projects during 2015 and 2016 respectively.

Improving access to justice for all and enhancing the rule of law have been critical priorities for Government and consequently in the last two decades specific initiatives were undertaken to extend access to justice – especially to the more rural areas. Many of you will be familiar with the new Legal Practice Act. In this Conference Call for Papers it refers to the Legal Practice Bill, as it then was, and states that "it is noteworthy that no mention has been made about paralegals in the present draft." The Bill has since been enacted and I can assure you that there is indeed specific mention of paralegal in the new Legal Practice Act. Section 34(9) of the Act provides that the Council must, within two years after the commencement of Chapter 2 of the Act, investigate and make recommendations to the Minister on the Statutory recognition of paralegals, taking into account best international practices, the public interest and the interests of the legal profession, with the view to legislative and other interventions in order to improve access to the legal profession and access to justice generally. This provision was inserted into the Legal Practice Bill by the portfolio Committee in the National Assembly after representations were received from paralegal organisations to ensure that provision was made for the finalisation of legislation. As it will take about three years for the Legal Practice Council to be established, we need to consider whether this is still the best way to go or whether work should not start earlier on legislation relating to paralegals.

We are aware of the problems being faced by paralegals, in particular issues of funding and formal recognition. For example, last week it was reported that the Paralegal Advice Office in Gugulethu will soon be forced to close down if it is unable to secure funding by April this year. Founded in 1998, the office has assisted hundreds of people with a variety of legal issues, ranging from consumer rights to social grant deductions and mediation matters. The office coordinator, a paralegal, Matthews Tshofuthi, said "at this stage we are running dry. I don't even know if we will be able to pay the telephone bill for January. The Ward Counsellor is helping us with the office we work from because we can't afford to pay rent." We know that many community paralegals, working in non-governmental organisations (NGO's), community advice offices and other grassroots institutions, face the same problem of struggling to get funding it needs to keep the projects going. Paralegals play a pivotal role not only in assisting people with issues such as housing benefits, social grants and consumer rights, but also importantly in the criminal justice process.

A 2010 World Bank report states that –

"Paralegal services should be viewed as especially necessary in Sub- Sahara Africa because of the poor extent of access to justice available to most Africans.

In systems suffering from high prisoner remand populations and extensive court delays, there can be little or no case for bolstering the private legal profession or even the government public defender offices while the more urgent need for paralegal services is neglected. Paralegals should be viewed as a priority in building credible systems of justice in Africa."

According to the December 2012 S A Crime Quarterly Inter-national legal and regulatory frameworks have supported the existence of paralegals as service providers in the crim-inal justice process since 2004. The Lilongwe Declaration on Accessing Legal Aid to the maximum number of persons must rely on paralegals.

The Lilongwe Declaration and its associates Plan of Action were adopted by the African Commission on Human and People's Rights in 2006 and by the UN Economic and Social Council (ECOSOC) in 2007. The United Nations Principles and Guidelines on Access to Legal Aid in Criminal Justice Systems urge states to recognise the role played by parale-gals in providing legal aid services.

According to the UN Principles it states, should in consul-tation with civil society, justice agencies and professional associations, introduce measures to develop a nationwide scheme of paralegal services with standardised training cur-ricula and accreditation schemes. States must also ensure that quality standards for paralegals services are set and that paralegals receive adequate training and operate under the supervision of qualified lawyers. States are encouraged to ensure access for accredited paralegals who are assigned to provide legal aid to police stations, facilities of detention, pre-trial detention centre and prisons and allow court ac-credited and duly trained paralegals to participate in court proceedings.

Dugard and Drage argue, in their article published in 2013, that –

"Although post-apartheid constitutional reforms guaran-teed a broad range of rights and benefits to all South Af-ricans, including the rights to legal assistance, accessing

many of these benefits remains a challenge for these who live in remote areas and these who cannot afford legal representation.

Community based paralegals fill this gap by providing dispute resolution and legal support that is both geographically and financially accessible and informed by a deep understanding of the social issues and everyday challenges facing their clients. Despite the prevalence and importance of paralegals in the South African Justice sector, their role remains, largely under-formalised and understudied.

They argue that without formal regulation or recognition, paralegals working in community advice offices face, what they describe as "the twin problems of insufficient funding and inadequate training."

These are some of the very vital aspects which will need to be discussed and debated in greater detail. When we embark on the process of creating specific legislation for paralegals.

And there are other important considerations too, for example a report by the Wits Justice project states that the paralegal landscape is undefined and the definition of a paralegal is broad, compared to other countries. South Africa has a varied practitioner group, that all identify themselves as paralegals. This raises the question of who is a paralegal. Is a person who might not have a formal qualification, but is doing invaluable work within a community a paralegal or not?

There is the issue of accountability. For example, who ensures that a paralegal gives reliable advice? How is the public going to hold paralegals accountable to the advice they give communities? And where do clients go to complain if a paralegal has rendered a bad service?

These are all the issues that need to be addressed in the very near future, if we envisage drafting specific legislation for the paralegal profession.

Ladies and Gentleman,

I wish you a very successful conference. I think what is important for all of us here today, practitioner, academics, civil society and us in government, is the question of how do we enhance and strengthen the position of paralegals.

Paralegals provide vital access to justice services and legal redress in our country. Having one of the most progressive Constitutions in the world means very little to communities if they are unaware of their rights or unaware of where to go for assistance in exercising these rights.

Every single paralegal in our country is able to better the human condition for others. They are skilled and able to assist in human rights struggles within their communities.

They can make justice a reality.

I thank you.

Issued by:
Department of Justice and Constitutional Development

INTRODUCTION: SOUTH AFRICAN LAW

South African Law is a combination of different legal systems, with its origin in Europe and Great Britain. Its foundation lies in Roman-Dutch Law, which is itself a blend of indigenous Dutch customary Law and Roman Law.

The Constitution of the Republic of South Africa, 1996 is the Supreme Law of the country and binds all legislative, executive and judicial organs of State at all levels of government. The judicial authority in South Africa is vested in the courts, which are independent and subject only to the Constitution and the law. No person or organ of State may interfere with the functioning of the courts, and an order or decision of a court binds all organs of State and people to whom it applies.

DIFFERENT COURTS

The Constitution provides for the following courts:

- Constitutional Court

- Supreme Court of Appeal (SCA)

- High Courts, including any High Court of Appeal that may be established by an Act of Parliament to hear appeals from High Courts

- Magistrates Court

- Any other court established or recognised in terms of an Act of Parliament, including any court of a status similar to either High Courts or Magistrates Courts.

Other courts also include:

- Labour Court

- Labour Appeal Court

- Land Claims Court

- Competition Appeal Court

- Electoral Court

- Divorce Court

- Small Claims Court

- Equality Court

- "Military Courts"

Decisions of the Constitutional Court, the Supreme Court of Appeal and the High Courts are an important source of law. These courts uphold and enforce the Constitution, which has an extensive Bill of Rights binding all state organs and all people.

The courts are also required to declare any law or conduct that is inconsistent with the Constitution to be invalid, and develop common law that is consistent with the values of the Constitution and the spirit and purpose of the Bill of Rights.

Source: South African Yearbook 2014/15 www.gov.za

CONSTITUTION OF SOUTH AFRICA

It always amazes me when I run courses and workshops how many paralegals do not understand how the Constitution of South Africa works. It is the very foundation of our country and should be studied and fully understood by any person who has studied or intends to study law.

I have kept to the very basics of our Constitution to give the readers key information rather than a chapter of legal rambling.

In 1994, after decades of living under an apartheid government, the first democratic election was held in South Africa. For the first time South Africa could call itself a democracy because everyone who was a citizen of South Africa could vote in the elections.

The Constitutional Assembly was constituted with the task of drawing up a constitution to represent the interests and needs of all the people of South Africa.

Included in the Constitution was a Bill of Rights which gave people rights and responsibilities.

WHAT IS A CONSTITUTION?

A Constitution of a country sets outs:

- The social values that the country believes in

- The structures of government

- What powers and authority a government and government bodies have

- The rights of citizens

- The relationship between government and citizens

- Aspects of the relationship between citizens

A Constitution is the highest law in the land and must be respected by all government bodies. It is higher than parliament and it can override any law that parliament makes if the law goes against the Constitution, whether it is a customary law or a law that parliament makes.

The South African Constitution of 1996 is a document that consists of 14 chapters. It states how the government should rule the country and it includes the Bill of Rights.

WHAT IS A DEMOCRACY?

Democracy means that everyone has a say about how the country is run. In a democracy, the government is put into power by its citizens.

The adult citizens of a democracy elect their government. One way they do this is by choosing people to represent them in parliament.

In a multi-party system, the party that gets the majority votes governs the country.

CHARACTERISTICS THAT IDENTIFY A DEMOCRACY

- Citizens can participate in government

- It is everyone's right and duty to participate in government

- All people are equal before the law

- There is no legal discrimination based on race, religion, gender or other reasons. Groups and individuals have a right to their own cultures, language, beliefs and so on

- Political tolerance – Various opinions, beliefs, cultures, religions and so on need to be tolerated. So, while the majority of the people rule in a democracy, the rights of the minority must still be protected

- Accountability – Officials that are elected and appointed in government are accountable to the people for actions and decisions

- Transparency – In a democracy people and the media can get information about what government decisions are being made, by whom and for what reason

- Regular, free and fair elections – Citizens choose their own representatives for government. They elect these officials in a free and fair way, without corruption and votes are secret

- Economic freedom – People can own property and businesses and they can choose their own work and join labour unions

- Controlling abuse of power – There must be ways to prevent government officials from abusing their power. The courts are independent from government, and there are other bodies that have the power to act against corrupt government officials

- Human rights – Democracies aim to respect and protect the human rights of all and after use the Bill of Rights to do so

- Multi-party system – A multi-party system means that more than one political party can participate in elections, so that people can choose who they want to represent them in government

- Rule of law – No one is above the law, including the president. This means that the law must treat everyone in a fair and equal manner

- The separation of powers between different arms of government – The Legislature (Parliament) is made up of people's representatives, who make the laws and policies. The Executive (Cabinet) implement and oversee the public service. The Judiciary act as independent referee's to interpret the law when there are disputes or conflicts or someone breaks the law

DEVELOPMENT OF CONSTITUTIONS IN SOUTH AFRICA

Between 1910 and 1994 there have been four Constitutions in South Africa:

- In 1910 Britain decided to withdraw from the government of South Africa and handed the country over to the white residents of the country who were the British settlers and Boers.

The first Constitution for the Union of South Africa was adopted in 1910. This gave rights to the white minority but took away the right to vote of the majority of South Africans.

- In 1960 the white government held a referendum to decide whether South Africa would become a Republic. On the 31 May 1961 South Africa was declared a Republic and the government adopted the second Constitution. This also took away the rights of black people

- In 1983 the government passed the third Constitution. This Constitution created the tri-cameral parliament, which meant there was a separate parliament for the white, coloured and Indian groups. This constitution excluded black people and automatically made them citizens of the homeland where they born. They had no rights outside these homelands

- In 1994, twenty- six parties negotiated and adopted an interim Constitution that gave voting rights to everyone and this Constitution lasted for two years

- During that time the elected government worked as the Constitutional Assembly and had to draw up a final Constitution. This finally became law on the 18th December 1996

CODESA

In February 1990, the National Party government un-banned political parties, released many political prisoners and detainees, and unbanned many people, including the late Nelson Mandela.

On the 20th and 21st December 1990 the first session of Codesa (Convention for a Democratic South Africa) was held. There were 19 political groups at this event.

All parties agreed to support the 'Declaration of Intent', which said that they would begin writing a new Constitution for South Africa.

THE MULTI-PARTY NEGOTIATING PROCESS.

In March 1993 full negotiations were initiated under the name of the MPNP (Multi-Party Negotiating Process instead of Codesa).

Twenty Six parties took part in the MPNP to write and adopt an interim Constitution to say how the government would govern after the elections on the 27th April 1994.

The MPNP drew up the interim Constitution which was to last for two years.

THE CONSTITUTIONAL ASSEMBLY (CA)

After the elections in 1994 the new parliament working as the Constitutional Assembly (CA) wrote the final Constitution and on the 8th May 1996, it was finally adopted by the Constitutional Assembly.

The final Constitution was passed by parliament and became law on the 18th December 1996.

THE SOUTH AFRICAN CONSTITUTION

The South African Constitution describes the social values of the country, and sets out the structures of government, what powers and authority a government has, and what rights citizens have.

The 'Founding Provisions' of the Constitution set out the principles and guarantees of democracy in South Africa.

Because the Constitution is the highest law in the land, it stops each new government from passing its own laws that contradict the Constitution.

It is also much more difficult to change the Constitution than any other law as it needs a two thirds majority vote in parliament.

THE CONSTITUTION THEREFORE PROTECTS DEMOCRACY IN SOUTH AFRICA

A government should never have unlimited power. Even governments which have been democratically elected can abuse the power that they have been given.

There are cases of governments who were elected in democratic elections and who then refused to allow further elections and became permanent rulers.

Other governments abuse their power by persecuting people who are against them.

IMPORTANT

The Constitution guards against governments in the future abusing the powers that they will have.

Our Constitution helps to guard against abuse of power by:

- Having rules about when elections should happen and what happens to parties that lose

- Making it difficult to change the Constitution

- Making sure that no person or government body has too much power

- The separation of powers (splitting power between different branches of government – parliament, cabinet and judiciary)

- Setting out the human rights that people have in a bill of Rights

- Creating independent courts and commissions that will protect people's rights, as well as monitor the government to make sure that is doing its work properly

- Making it compulsory for all government bodies to be accountable and transparent to the public

THE RELATIONSHIP BETWEEN THE CONSTITUTION AND OTHER LAWS

The Constitution is a law passed by parliament and it is the highest law in the land. All other laws must follow it. Other laws are divided into statutes (laws or acts), common law and customary law.

Statutes are laws or acts which are made by government. Laws made by the national parliament are called 'acts of parliament', laws made by the provincial legislatures are called 'ordinances' and laws made by the municipal councils are called 'by-laws'.

CHAPTER 1

"The ones, who are crazy enough to think they can change the world, are the ones that do."

– STEVE JOBS

LEGAL PRACTITIONERS

The legal profession is divided into two branches –

- Advocates

- Attorneys

  – that is subject to strict ethical codes.

Advocates are organised into Bar Associations or Societies, one each at the seat of the various divisions of the High Court. There are voluntary associations of Advocates such as the General Council of the Bar of South Africa and the formations of independent bars.

There are four regional societies for attorneys, each made up of a number of provinces. A practicing attorney is ipso jure (by the operation of law) a member of at least one of these societies, which seek to promote the interests of the profession. The Law Society of South Africa is a voluntary association established to coordinate the various regional societies. In terms of the Right of Appearance, in Courts Act, 1995 (Act 62 of 1995), Advocates can appear in any court, while attorneys may be heard in all of the country's lower courts and can also acquire the right of appearance in the superior courts. The Attorneys Amendment Act, 1993 (At 115 of 1993), provides for alternative routes for admission as an attorney. All attorneys who hold an LLB or equivalent degree, or who have at least three year's experience, may acquire the right of audience in the High Court.

Source South Africa Yearbook 2014/15 www.gov.za

FORMAL RECOGNITION OF PARALEGALS IN THE LEGAL SYSTEM

The public and the legal profession recognise that paralegals are important because they allow people to have access to justice. However, for many years paralegals were not formally recognised by the legal profession.

There are a number of regulatory options being considered for paralegals, including an independent regulatory framework.

*"The mind is not just a vessel to be filled,
but a fire to be ignited."*

- PLUTARCH

THE TRUE MEANING OF "PARALEGAL"

DEFINITION 1

Adjective:

Relating to auxiliary aspects of the law

Noun:

A person trained in subsidiary legal matters but not fully qualified as a lawyer

DEFINITION 2

The prefix "Para" is used for something that is separate from the word it's next too but still related to it. A paraprofessional for example helps other professionals, like teachers, but isn't actually a teacher. Paralegals are not lawyers, but they assist lawyers.

A paralegal is part of the support team for attorneys.

You will note that the base of the triangle is much larger than the next two levels. Therefore it must be noted how important the paralegal and support team are to the attorneys and law firms.

CHAPTER 3

"Maybe it is simply about having that huge vision and remaining single minded to make it happen."

– UNKNOWN

WHAT DOES IT MEAN TO BE A PARALEGAL IN SOUTH AFRICA?

Which brings to me why I have chosen to write a book that assists the South African Paralegal to understand what it takes to be a successful paralegal and enjoy the legal world as much as an attorney or advocate. There are so many opportunities in our country for paralegals but nobody has taken the time to lead the way in this field. Paralegals are seen to be cheap labour and "want to be" attorneys but that is so far from the truth! We are not just assistants, filing clerks, secretaries, coffee makers and personal assistants.

The true paralegal is someone who loves law just as much as anybody else does and wants to play a part in making a difference. We understand the law just as well as any other legal practitioner. Paralegals are used for researching matters and a paralegal worth his/her salt will know the case studies as well as his/her boss, in actual fact I have come across paralegals that can recite case studies better and in more depth than most legal practitioners, so why then are paralegals seen as nothing better than a cheap labourer. I am hoping to change this perception of paralegals and set out to prove that a good paralegal is worth more than just a pay check. Of course it will also take for the paralegal to increase their knowledge and professionalism in the industry.

And the big question should be, how? Well, I have found the following points to be invaluable to a paralegal who wants to advance in his/her company or the paralegal who wants to start their own freelance business.

- Knowledge – is the first key to success. Study, study and then study some more. Depending on which area of law interests you, follow every story, read every bit of material you can lay your hands on relating to your area of interest. I.e. the Oscar Pretorius case for criminal law paralegals has been a smorgasbord of interesting twists and turns

- Paperwork – must be in the most impeccable order

- Attitude – If you want to stay a paralegal then keep the paralegal attitude, I promise you it won't let you down. But if you want more - nothing says it more than attitude!

- Confidence – with the right attitude will come confidence and I don't mean being a smart ass, I mean being somebody that others look up to

- Learn to understand people – enrol on psychology course, get to know human behaviour

- Dress code – Dress better than the boss, this will certainly lift eyebrows at the office. When we feel good we do well! Spend more money on how you look than on social activities in the beginning stages and watch how you will be treated. With looking and feeling good will come the attitude and confidence that will shoot you up the scales of acceptance.

A PARALEGAL IS A PERSON, WHO

- Has basic knowledge of the law and its procedures

- Knows about conflict resolution procedures

Paralegals use their knowledge and experience to help people with legal and other problems.

A paralegal may investigate and refer matters to attorneys or relevant bodies for them to deal with. They can also become educators on the law and rights for people in their communities.

Paralegals are not just mini-attorneys. Obviously they cannot assist people in court and other tribunals until they acquire the relevant qualification and accreditation.

But more than this their role is to look at a variety of methods, other than using the courts, to achieve long-term, sustainable solutions to people's problems.

Using the courts can bring quick relief which is important in many cases, but this is not always the case. Court cases can take a long time to be finalised, the costs involved are often huge and the outcome for a person may be negative.

PARALEGALS SHOULD AIM TO DEAL WITH PROBLEMS IN A MORE HOLISTIC WAY

EXAMPLE

- A woman and her children, who are suffering from abuse at the hands of the husband and father, should be advised by a paralegal to apply for a Protection Order. But the paralegal should also see the bigger picture. The woman and her children are financially dependent on the husband and father for their survival so they cannot move out of the house unless they are supported in this process.

- The paralegal should therefore help the woman apply for Child Support Grants for her children and she should be referred to Child Welfare or to a woman's abuse organisation for support.

IMPORTANT NOTE

In general, a paralegal should focus more on the use of conflict resolution methods like negotiation, conciliation, mediation and arbitration to resolve conflict rather than using the courts.

COUNSELLING SKILLS

Sometimes people just want to talk to you about their problems and it may not be necessary for you to take any further action. It might be enough for you to counsel someone about ways to deal with a problem.

Counselling is a skill used mainly by professional psychologists and social welfare employees. Where the issues raised by an advice seeker can have serious psychological consequences (for example, in the case of a child who has been abused, raped etc) they will need deeper counselling.

IMPORTANT NOTE

Paralegals are not trained to provide this service so they should refer the person to a professional.

REFERRALS

Paralegals often play an important role by linking people with a problem to an appropriate agency that is more qualified and better trained to deal with the problem.

Always give the person a covering letter when you refer him or her to another organisation or attorney. Explain why you are referring the person to them and what work, if any, you have done on the case.

I have always made sure that I look like a million dollars when meeting clients or at court in front of other legal practitioners. The passages of the courts are like walking on a modelling ramp. YOU WILL ALWAYS GET NOTICED!

Many of my clients are people who have noticed me at court assisting people or court officials. Never under estimate the value of a good wardrobe.

CHAPTER 4

"Stamp your creative impression on everything and make it the agent of your will, the executor of your purpose."

– ZECHARIAH FENDEL

THE DO'S AND DONT'S OF A PARALEGAL

THE DO'S

- Be inquisitive – don't take things at face value! Research is of most importance

- Make sure you treat everybody with the respect you would expect

- Only open your mouth when you have something worth saying or of any importance

- Have an open mind

- Listen and learn

- Be prepared for all meetings

- Work longer hours than anybody else, arrive first and leave last.

THE DONT'S

- Never ever refer to yourself as an attorney

- Never ever give advice that does not fall within your paralegal status.

- Never leave clients believing that you are more than a paralegal

- Never promise anything that you cannot support

- Never use legal words that you don't fully understand

- Never ever breach the parameters set by your superior

- Never use foul language to put your point across (even if you know the person)

CHAPTER 5

"Keep affirmations where you can see them."

– JOHAN CLAASSENS

JOB DESCRIPTION OF A PARALEGAL

- Conduct client interviews and maintain contact with clients

- Prepare legal documents, pleadings and correspondence

- Perform legal research

- Locate and interview potential witnesses

- Conduct and/or organise investigations and document searches

- Review and summarise discovery

- Attend court and procedural meetings, such as estate planning meetings with clients

- Author independent work-related correspondence

A paralegal specialist is one that is not easily nailed down to a one page description – one size fits all – because paralegal positions will vary depending on the paralegal work and what area of law they practice in. But there are some basic duties that most paralegals should be prepared to perform.

CHAPTER 6

"Wisdom is like a baobab tree; no one can embrace it."

– AFRICAN PROVERB

PARALEGAL DUTIES

Duties for private sector paralegals range from more difficult tasks such as legal research to tasks more administrative in nature.

REQUIREMENTS

- Perform legal and factual research

- Perform research of records

- Identify relevant judicial decisions, statutes, legal articles, codes and other pertinent material

- Organise and analyse information

- Cross- check and validate information

- Prepare written reports

- Draft legal documents including briefs, appeals, wills, contracts and legal agreements

- Help prepare legal arguments, applications, declarations and motions

- Prepare correspondence

- Check legal forms and documents for accuracy

- Maintain reference files

- Organise and track case files

- Review and monitor new and updated regulations

- Co-ordinate law office activities such as subpoena delivery

- Find and communicate with witnesses

- Interview and interact with clients

- Assist attorneys in depositions

"Do just once do what others say you can't do, and you will never pay attention to their limitations again."

– JAMES R. COOK

PARALEGAL RESPONSIBILITIES

In the public sector, responsibilities of a paralegal are broad. Litigation paralegals help manage files, complete research and analyse evidence for hearings. Paralegals who work for the government may also research their agencies policies and regulations.

In community service areas, paralegals will have more direct contact with clients. Paralegals in this area will interview clients, conduct research and prepare and file documents for the agencies under privileged clients.

These are some of the needs that paralegals can provide:

- Give legal and general advice to people on the law and their rights

- Write and distribute pamphlets, booklets and other resources to help educate people

- Refer people to social and health services, and other helpful organisations

- Refer people to attorneys where it is clear an attorney is necessary

- Help prepare people for legal procedures, such as what to expect in a court case

- Assist and prepare to take labour problems to the Commission for Conciliation, Mediation and Arbitration (CCMA)

- Run workshops to educate people about their rights

- Work as a link between a community and attorneys, and assist with things like taking statements, interpreting and follow up on cases

- Build contacts with other paralegals, resources and organisations regionally and nationally

IMPORTANT

Paralegals play an important role in the legal process because many people cannot afford attorneys or at times find it intimidating going to an attorney.

"Success is sweet but the secret is sweat."

– ROBINS FREEDOM

DESIRED PARALEGAL SKILLS

- Research skills

- Analytical skills

- Critical thinking skills

- Organisational skills

- Strong communication skills

- Stress tolerance

- Detail orientated

- Computer skills

*"We are what we repeatedly do. Excellence, then,
is not an act, but a habit."*

– ARISTOTLE

TYPES OF PARALEGALS

If you desire to become a paralegal, you may want to really hunker down and decide what type of paralegal you are interested in being. Some of the paralegal areas are broken down here for your consideration:

- Litigation

- Immigration

- Freelance (Contract)

- Corporate

- Bankruptcy

- Real estate

- Family Law

- Intellectual Property

- Criminal

A freelance paralegal is also known as a contract paralegal that works independently and assists lawyers on a case by case basis. If you are a paralegal who is working for a firm and considering starting your business or looking to expand your business into additional types of paralegal jobs.

CHAPTER 10

"To dream anything you want to dream, that is the beauty of the human mind. To do anything that you want to do, that is the strength of the human will. To trust yourself, to test your limits that is the courage to succeed."

– BERNARD EDMONDS

HOW TO BUILD YOUR PARALEGAL BUSINESS

If you are considering opening your own paralegal business, there are certain details you should consider before opening your doors. As with any small business, a freelance paralegal should begin with a strong foundation for a successful business.

FORMULATE A BUSINESS PLAN

Writing down your business plan helps you visualise how you will begin your paralegal business as well as the direction you want to take your business in the future. In your business plan, include the following sections.

COMPANY DESCRIPTION

This should describe what paralegal services you will offer the market you want to service and what makes your business different from other paralegal services.

ORGANISATION AND MANAGEMENT SECTION

This should cover how you will organise and manage your business. If you intend having employees, you must determine the management structure you will use and how you will delegate work.

MARKETING

In order to be successful, you must have a marketing plan. How will attorneys find out about your services and how will you communicate with the market area? You should also include a growth strategy to build your business.

FUNDING AND FINANCIAL PROJECTIONS

If you need to borrow money to begin your business, this section should lay out a plan for obtaining funding. It must include your current funding requirements and how you intend to use the funds. Also, include a section with financial projections based on the amount of time you are committing to this business and the expected rate of pay for your paralegal services.

DETERMINE YOUR BUSINESS LOCATION

If you intend to work out of your home, you must set up your home office and equip it with necessary furniture and office equipment required to operate your business. You must consider how your family life might encroach on your business and how to keep both separate within your home. Operating a successful business from home requires discipline and organisation. If you intend to lease an office, consider the cost involved in rental payments, taxes, insurance and IT connections.

FINANCING YOUR BUSINESS

Until you can secure your first contract paralegal job, you will need to cover both business and paralegal costs, unless, you already have your foot in the door with law firms or several attorneys; it will take some time to establish clients. A smart business owner will have start up capital to cover expenses until the business begins to generate a profit. As a contract paralegal offering paralegal services, you may experience ebbs and flows in your business. Have a plan in place in case you must finance your business during slow periods.

MEET WITH AN ATTORNEY

Unless you are a paralegal that has extensive experience in corporate law, it would be advisable to meet with an attorney to discuss the type of legal structure for your paralegal business. There are advantages and disadvantages to being a sole proprietor, partnership, Limited Liability Company or a corporation. In order to determine the best ownership structure for your business, you should consult an attorney. In addition to assisting you determine the legal structure of your business; an attorney can also assist you with registering your business name.

CONSULT WITH AN ACCOUNTANT

Before making a final decision about the legal structure of your business, you should know in advance what type of self- employment taxes you may be required to pay for owning your own business.

DEVELOP A WEBSITE

With attorneys using technology more today than ever, it is important that your paralegal business has a website. In addition to an excellent marketing tool, your website is a means of communication with clients.

Staring a paralegal service business is a good investment for the paralegal who desires to own their own business and be their own boss. With hard work and dedication, you can build a successful freelance paralegal business that provides services to attorneys and to the public.

CHAPTER 11

"Time is the iron that smooth's away all the wrinkles in our past."

– VIBIN J. CHOWALLUR

MUST HAVES IN A BUSINESS PLAN

Making a living as a freelance or independent paralegal is essentially the same thing as running any small business. Being a professional in the legal field however, does not necessarily mean you will prosper as a small business owner. There is a completely different skill set that one must possess, or learn, to run a profitable freelance paralegal business.

More than half of all start up businesses fail due to poor business planning or the failure to correctly identify and manage potential risks, making a business plan is vital even to the already established business. There is a very common myth that only start up businesses need a business plan. In actuality, you should be reviewing and updating your business plan on an annual basis. Many big, well known companies call this an operational, strategic or annual plan. No matter what you choose to call it, your freelance paralegal business cannot afford not to have one.

WHAT SHOULD YOUR BUSINESS PLAN INCLUDE?

1. EXECUTIVE SUMMARY

The executive summary is the first page of a business plan but it should always be written last. It sums up everything and tells the reader what and where your business is, where you plan to take it, and why your business will be successful. The executive summary should be extremely persuasive

2. ELEVATOR PITCH

An elevator pitch is a brief description of your business. This should include the nature of your business, your target audience, the need your services will meet and what makes your freelance paralegal business unique.

Take your time when planning an elevator pitch for your business. It should be compelling and memorable. You can use the elevator pitch in many situations, for example, to tell people what you do for a living or to introduce your organisation.

Practice your elevator pitch on a regular basis. The manner in which it is delivered is as important as the words you use. You want it to sound natural.

3. MISSION STATEMENT

A mission statement very briefly states the purpose for your business and reflects its values. The ideal length of a mission statement is two to three sentences. A mission statement may seem unimportant, however, it is an extremely significant element of any successful business. A good mission statement should convey the values of your business, lead employees in the right direction and inspire potential clients. It should be an accurate representation of your company culture; a sense of identity. Keep your mission statement short and sweet.

4. GOALS AND OBJECTIVES

Setting and reaching short and long term goals is the hallmark of any thriving business; making business goals and objectives a key element of an annual business plan. Long term goals should be much more substantially greater than short term goals; taking anywhere from five to twenty years to reach. Defining your business goals require quite a bit of thought and most importantly, honesty. Be specific as possible to increase the chances of achieving your goals. As short term goals are achieved and new ones set, update this section of your annual business plan.

5. STRENGTHS AND WEAKNESSES

Strengths and weaknesses are not included in a traditional, formal business plan. But analysing your strengths and weaknesses each year and including them in on an annual business plan will benefit your freelance paralegal business in several ways. Identifying your businesses strength can help determine which future opportunities to pursue and where improvement is needed

6. KEY PERFORMANCE INDICATORS

Key performance indicators are a type of performance measurement that can be used to evaluate the success of a particular activity or overall success of the business. Examples of a key performance indicator include a number of new client acquisitions, the number of visitors that filled out your contact form. By identifying the KPI's that you will track in your business and listing them in this section of your annual business plan, you will be able to monitor how your business is performing and find potential problem areas before income is lost.

7. MARKETING STRATEGY

It is recommended that you create a comprehensive marketing plan that explains your marketing strategy in detail. Summarise your marketing plan for inclusion in your annual business plan.

8. FINANCIAL PROJECTIONS

Financial projections are required for small businesses to show financial institutions and potential creditors when seeking funding. Be realistic when filling in projected numbers. It never benefits anyone when financial projections are unrealistic. However, financial projections will also help you to understand more about your business and where it's heading.

Every month use true financial figures from the previous month's business to update and correct your financial projections. Creating an annual business plan will enable you to easily re-evaluate the most critical aspects of your free-lance paralegal business. By reassessing these aspects of your business on a regular basis you will greatly increase the chances of success.

Credit: Shelley Risiden

"I always knew I was going to be rich. I don't think I ever doubted it for a minute."

– WARREN BUFFETT

SEVEN STEPS TO SUCCESS

Should you want to freelance as a paralegal I believe the following points are imperative to follow:

1. Make sure you have served some form of internship with a law firm or attorney

2. Have a library of law books to research from

3. Make sure that this is the path you want to follow as a career (any doubts will make it a short career)

4. Believe in yourself and never let fear enter into your head

5. Have enough cash flow to keep you going for at least 3 months

6. Know your market and make a decision as to which area of law you want to assist in

7. Record keeping is of utmost importance

"Always bear in mind that your own resolution to success is more important than any other one thing."

– ABRAHAM LINCOLN

STRATEGY

What does strategy really mean?

"Being strategic" requires a sense of confidence in one's decision making process which cannot be founded on 100 percent proof of concept.

"Being strategic" means being perceptive future-orientated, open minded, proactive, working off the front-foot, and making and taking decisions based on evidence and calculated hunches.

A good strategy provides a clear roadmap, consisting of a set of guiding principles or rules, that defines the actions people in business should take (and not take) and the things they should prioritise (and not prioritise) to achieve desired goals.

As such, a strategy is just one element of the overall strategic direction that leaders must define for their businesses.

Strategy is about <u>how</u> resources should be allocated to accomplish the mission.

One straightforward implication is that you can't develop a strategy for your business without first thinking through missions and goals.

Strategy can also be defined as "a general direction set for your business and its various components to achieve a desired state in the future".

Strategy, in short, bridges the gap between "where are we" and "where we want to be."

Michael Porter developed three generic strategies, that a business could use to gain a competitive advantage, back in 1980.

They are:-

- Cost Leadership

- Differentiation

- Focus

COST LEADERSHIP

The cost leadership strategy advocates gaining competitive advantage of the lowest cost of a product or service. Lowest cost need not mean lowest price.

"Costs are removed from every link of the value chain".

The service could still be priced at competitive parity (same price as others), but because of lower cost of production (your services), your business would be able to sustain itself even through lean times and invest more into the business all throughout.

DIFFERENTIATION

Strategy involves creation of differentiated services. A variety of services, each branded and promoted differently, with levels of function, which allows your business to "desensitize" prices, and on the basis of being different, charge premium or higher rates.

This strategy also provides a hedge against different markets, allowing cash flow to come in even if other market area's grow or mature.

FOCUS

Definition of focus:

- The centre of interest or activity

- The state or quality of having or producing clear visual definition

- Strategy involves focusing on a narrow, defined segment of the market, also called a 'niche' segment.

- A business in a niche market has clients who understand, appreciate and can pay a premium for their indulgence.

- Competitive advantage, either by cost or differentiation is created specially, for the niche. But, the risks are that the niche may not grow, or it may disappear with time and change.

CHAPTER 14

"Finding inner strength looking beyond the visible and focusing life's search on the unseen."

- UNKNOWN

PURPOSE

DEFINITION OF PURPOSE

- The reason for which something is done or created

- A person's sense of resolve or determination

- Have as one's intention or objective

WHAT IS LIFE PURPOSE?

Your life purpose consists of the central motivating aims of your life – The reasons you get up in the mornings.

Purpose can guide life decisions, influence behaviour, shape goals, offer a sense of direction, and create meaning.

Purpose will be unique for everyone; what you identify as your path may be different from others.

What's more, your purpose can actually shift and change throughout life in response to the evolving priorities and fluctuations of your own experiences.

"Genuine purpose points to the end of a self-absorbed, self-serving, relationship to life."

When your authentic purpose becomes clear, you will be able to share it with the whole world.

60

"YOUR LIFE PURPOSE IS YOUR CONTRIBUTION"

CHAPTER 15

"He who believes is strong; he who doubts is weak. Strong convictions precede great actions."

— LOUISA MAY ALCOTT

GOAL SETTING

Goal setting is the process of deciding what you want to accomplish and devising a plan to achieve the result you desire.

For effective goal setting, you need to do more than just decide what you want to do; you also have to work at accomplishing whatever goal you have set.

There are 3 types of goals:

- Outcome goals

- Process goals

- Performance goals

Each of the 3 types differ based on how much control we have over it.

We have the most control over process goals and the least control over outcome goals.

There are 5 keys to effective goal setting:

- Develop a clear vision. While it might seem obvious, knowing what you hope to accomplish is seminal to achieving your goal.

- Write down your goals

- Get things done

- Keep your eye on the prize

- Review, Assess, Repeat

Goal setting is based on the premise that much human action is purposeful, in that it is directed by conscious goals. (O'Neil and Drillings,1994,p.14)

The decision to set goals results from dissatisfaction with current performance levels.

Setting goals should include setting a structure that directs actions and behaviours which improve the unsatisfactory performance.

Setting a goal will change a person's behaviour in order to work towards achieving the set goal.

Goal setting predicts that people will channel effort towards accomplishing their goals, which will in turn affect performance. (Locke and Latham, 2006)

CHAPTER 16

"Vision gives purpose, somewhere to go. It's the compass that keeps us going in the right direction; the blue print with which we build tomorrow today."

– UNKNOWN

EPI- CENTER

DEFINITION

The point on the earth's surface that is directly above the focus (the point of origin) of an earthquake.

The epi-center is usually the location where the greatest damage is associated when an earthquake occurs.

We as paralegals are sitting right on top of the epi-center of law.

The belly of law is starting to rumble.

Soon the volcano of law will erupt bringing with it a ripple effect, the magnitude never seen before!

DESTINATION (MANAGEMENT)

DEFINITION

- The place to which someone or something is going or being sent

- Denoting a place that people will make a special trip or being sent

Destination management is the co-ordinated management of all elements that make up a destination.

An effective (DM) is extremely essential for developing, managing and promoting a destination over specific period of time.

Setting clear plans of action and allocating resources.

"IT'S IN YOUR DNA"

"That quality that separates you from everyone. Your natural and unique ability. Take that and combine it with your unlimited potential to move towards success, you will get exponential results."

CHAPTER 17

"Happy people don't go through life collecting recognition. They go through life giving it away."

– DODINSKY

NETWORKING FOR BUSINESS

I am always asked the following question, *"where do I begin to get business"*? My answer always stays the same. Network and more networking! As a paralegal you really need to spend time proving that you have ability and understanding to assist people with the filling in of forms. This will go a long way in referral business. Once you have the confidence you can start offering your services to assist people in approaching the various courts and following through to the time that the file has to be handed over to an attorney for further instructions. It is very important that you make sure that you have a relationship with an attorney/s you believe to be good and competent as this will be a reflection on your service levels to the client. The client will always want your undertaking that the attorney you have referred will take care of them the same way you did when you assisted them with their paperwork. The attorney must also be confident in your abilities and feel that you are professional enough to allow you to assist them in going forward. Once you build a relationship with an attorney this should give you the confidence to enjoy being an assistant in very important legal work.

Having a network of professional contacts and colleagues will be a huge advantage in today's working world. It gives you a support system full of people who do the same type of work you do. It provides a group of knowledgeable people to contact if you have any questions, concerns or need to refer someone to obtain a reference.

HOW DOES ONE BUILD THEIR PROFESSIONAL NETWORK?

Here are 3 simple steps to help augment your career with a strong network of legal professionals.

TAKE ADVANTAGE OF TRAINING TIME

Whether you are still in paralegal college or taking workshops to advance your paralegal career, use that time wisely to get to know the people around you. You never know if a fellow paralegal student may continue on to law school or become a paralegal employer years down the road, or if the person sitting next to you at seminar may work at a law firm where you have been wanting to interview. Also, making friends with your fellow students means you have a group of people to commiserate with when you have a tough assignment, and people to encourage and congratulate you along your career path. Engage with people around you, make friends and exchange contact information whenever you are in a time of training for your paralegal career.

JOIN PROFESSIONAL NETWORKS AND ATTEND EVENTS

There are myriads of national and local professional associations you can join, and these associations host networking events, seminars, workshops, conventions and fun parties. There is no reason not to join and attend events. Push yourself out of your comfort zone, make small talk, exchange business cards, add to your paralegal knowledge, and make new friends!

USE SOCIAL MEDIA

With today's technology, you don't have to be a wiz with small talk to be a great networker. Social media has made professional networking even easier. Many people use Facebook and Twitter to network, but the primary professional networking platform of all social media sites is LinkedIn.

THROUGH YOUR NETWORK, YOU CAN

- Be discovered for business opportunities

- Gain new insights from joining discussions with other professionals

- Discover inside connections that can help you find a work position

- Join groups related to your desired area of interest

You don't have to be an expert or bang down people's doors to grow your paralegal network and ultimately advance your paralegal career. You simply have to make a little effort to connect with fellow professionals around you, whether in college, at professional events or online.

Credit: Katie Fridsma

CHAPTER 18

"The very best way to create the future is to create it."

– MICHAEL KAMI

NETWORKING CONTINUED

Not to be confused with marketing, networking refers to building relationships with others. Networking may lead to increased business for your paralegal services practice and can help you avoid isolating yourself to the detriment of your health and your business. Networking can also provide broader benefits, which may include the opportunity to connect with –

- mentors, to assist or to guide you in your practice

- mentees, to share the benefits of your own experiences

- other professionals, to exchange services or referrals

- prospective employees, to help support your practice

- prospective employers or clients to engage your services

- your community, to build friendships and support

Though the benefits of any particular networking relationship may not be immediate, any paralegal opening a legal services practice should consider networking to increase visibility both professionally and personally.

CONSIDER PROSPECTIVE CONTACTS FOR YOUR NETWORKING, INCLUDING –

- continuing legal education or professional development initiatives, as a speaker or participant

- friends, family and neighbours

- volunteer, associations and religious affiliations

- former professors and classmates

- sports teams and health club members

- colleagues and other contacts

- former and existing clients

- consider using the services offered by these in your network and referring others to do the same

- re-evaluate your methods, as you become more comfortable with networking

- schedule time to develop and maintain your network

CHAPTER 19

*"It's not what we do once in a while that shapes
our lives. It's what we do consistently."*

– ANTHONY ROBBINS

TOUTING

DEFINITION

- Attempt to sell (something), typically by a direct or persistent approach

- Attempt to persuade people of the merits of a service

The Law Society of the Northern Provinces (LSNP) has provided some guidance on advertising and marketing in its 'Advertising and Marketing Guidelines.'

These, however, specifically state that nothing in the rules will insist that a firm directly or indirectly take part in touting.

Although these guidelines are descriptive, I submit that they are insufficient.

The guidelines state that touting includes –

- Soliciting customer or work directly from any person

- Entering into an arrangement with any person, whether an employee or not, for the introduction of clients to the attorney; but this will not apply to –

» Any arrangement between an attorney and another attorney for the referral of work in the normal course of either's practice;

» Any arrangement for the introduction to an attorney of other attorneys with a view to their instructing him on an agency basis;

» Making unsolicited visits or telephone calls or sending unsolicited letters or printed material to any person (other than to an existing professional connection) whom the attorney knows or should reasonably be expected to know has an existing attorney/client relationship with another attorney, where such conduct is carried out with a view to, or is calculated to, establishing an attorney/client or correspondent relationship with such person.

Further, the rules of the LSNP provide that 'touting for work of a professional nature includes' –

• Accepting or agreeing to accept or offering to accept re-numeration for professional work at less than the tariffs of fees fixed by statute or regulation or rule; or

• By his/her conduct directly or indirectly holding himself/herself out as being prepared to do professional work at less than such tariff unless he/she proves that he/she did not do so with the objective of attracting work or business;

• Advertising in any manner in which the public is invited to entrust professional work to him/her or in which he/she holds himself/herself or his/her firm out as being prepared or qualified to do such work.

Credit – (Edrick Roux LLB (UP) www.derebus.org.za

A paralegal on the other hand has no restrictions when it comes to 'touting' for business.

As an agent not limited by any law the paralegal is in a superb position to look for clients and business without the fear of being reported to any authorities, as long as you do not mislead people into thinking that you are an attorney.

CHAPTER 20

"All growth is a leap in the dark, a spontaneous unpre-meditated act without benefit of experience."

– HENRY MILLAR

OUTSOURCING

WHY IS OUTSOURCING A GOOD BUSINESS STRATEGY?

It improves efficiency, cuts costs, speeds up product development and allows companies to focus on their "core competencies."

It enables an organisation to achieve business objectives, add value, tap into a resource base and mitigate risk.

Top 10 reasons why companies outsource:-

1. Lower operational and labour costs are among the primary reasons why companies choose to outsource. When properly executed it has a defining impact on a company's revenue recognition and can deliver significant savings.

2. Companies also choose to outsource so that they may continue focusing on their core business processes while delegating mundane time consuming processes to external agencies.

3. Outsourcing also enables companies to tap into and leverage a global knowledge base, having access to world class capabilities.

4. Freeing up internal resources that could be put into effective use for other purposes is also one of the primary benefits realized when companies outsource.

5. Many times stranded with internal resource crunches, many world class enterprises outsource to gain access to resources not available internally.

6. Outsourcing, many a time is undertaken to save costs and provide a capital buffer fund to companies that could be leveraged in a manner that best profits the company.

7. By delegating responsibilities to external agencies, companies can wash their hands off functions that are difficult to manage and control while still realizing their benefits.

8. Outsourcing helps companies mitigate risk and is also among the primary reasons embarked upon them.

9. Outsourcing also enables companies to realize the benefits of re-engineering, revise, and upgrade the project as per the client's requirements

10. Some companies also outsource to help them expand and gain access to new market areas, by taking the point of production or service delivery closer to their users.

Among additional reasons to outsource, companies undertake outsourcing for a variety of reasons depending upon their vision and purpose of the exercise.

While this may vary from company to company, the fruits of labour are visible among some of the leading enterprises world- wide, where outsourcing has become a core component of day to day business strategies.

Key reasons to look for in a company when suggesting outsourcing.

- Control operating costs

- Lower infrastructure investments

- Focus on core functions

- Accelerate migration to new technology

- Get access to world class capabilities and improve operational performance

- One time applications

- Overcome seasonal workflows

- Overcome talent shortages

- Enhance risk management

OUTSOURCING AS A BUSINESS MODEL

Though there has been a lot of controversies regarding outsourcing, the overwhelming advantages of outsourcing speak for themselves.

More companies are drawing up plans to outsource work.

Many companies now base their entire business plan around the delegation of functions to external service providers.

According to some experts, outsourcing is not simply a way of cutting costs; it is a new business model.

The trend is clearly in favour of outsourcing large volumes of work.

Vendors are moving up the value chain to include in their service offerings a range of additional services that require greater skills, research support, and expertise.

As vendors become more streamlined and improve on the outsourcing model, it is not difficult to see why outsourcing is here to stay.

CHAPTER 21

"Sow a thought, reap an action, sow an action, reap a habit, sow a habit, reap a character, sow a character, and reap a destiny."

– UNKNOWN

SERVICE RETAINER

A service retainer fee is an amount of money paid upfront to secure the services of a consultant, freelancer, lawyer, or other professionals.

It is most commonly paid to individual third parties that have been engaged by the payer to perform a specific action on their behalf.

The client pays a lump sum upfront, or makes a recurring monthly payment, and you work with them on a long-term project, or provide them with access to services each month.

Retainer agreements can bring stability to your business.

Listing everything included in the retainer fee manages your client's expectations and helps them plan their goals, based on the value you will bring to them.

If you go above and beyond every month (while still maintaining profitability, of course), work to deliver clients the value you have outlined, and show them how much peace of mind you bring.

SELL VALUE, NOT HOURS

CHAPTER 22

"Strength and growth come only through continuous effort and struggle"

– NAPOLEON HILL

ETHICS IN A BUSINESS ENVIRONMENT

ETHICS IS DEFINED AS:

- Professional ethics concerns itself with the rules that regulates professional conduct (Lala Camerer, African Security Review, Volume 5 no.6; 1996)

- The moral standards and principles that are applied to business relationships and activities

Any kind of business is based on relationships and interactions with people. This includes interaction with:

- Fellow colleagues

- Customers/clients

- Stakeholders

- Investors

- The community

According to Willem Landman, CEO of Ethics Institute of SA, there are five concepts that capture the essence of ethics, that is:

- Values – Values are sets of norm, standards, characteristics or ideas that shape what is right or wrong, what is good or bad. Organizational values proclaim what is expected from individuals and how they should behave. Basic ethical values include honesty, integrity and respect.

- Obligations – An obligation is a formal commitment concerning discharging our duties. These duties can be moral, legal, financial or social.

- Rights – Rights are described by Specialized Encyclopaedia and dictionaries are 'entitlements assured by custom, law or property'.

- Consequences – Every decision made, every action taken has consequences. Consequences can be good or bad. It is our ethical responsibility when doing business to promote consequences that are good and benefit organizations, clients and the community, and to avoid or reduce bad consequences that are harmful to the organization, client and community

- Character – This is an intrinsic quality that defines who we are. A person of good character finds it easy to take ethical decisions.

Good ethical behaviour depends on how much we base our actions and decisions on good values, whether we honour our obligations and whether we respect the rights of others.

As Willem Landman mentioned, these five concepts forms the core of 'ethics of business', and they should apply to all workers and professionals, as well as each business in South Africa.

Ethical business contact is based on basic principle of:

- Honesty and Integrity – Conducting business honestly, not giving false information, misleading information or lying

- Fairness – Being sensitive to the sense of justice

- Respect – Treating all with respect and courtesy

- Accountability – Taking responsibility of consequences of one's actions, whether right or wrong

- Disclosure – Providing accurate and complete information up-front, so as not to mislead clients, communities and stakeholders in a business transaction

- Confidentiality – Treating the organizations' and clients information with respect, and divulging it irresponsibly

- Respect of diversity – Acknowledging people's diverse cultures, race and way of doing things

Absence of business ethics leads to:

- Corruption

- Maladministration

- Poor service delivery

- Fraud

"Today I shall look for opportunities in my own 'garden'. The grass may look greener elsewhere, but it will have been just as hard to cut."

– UNKNOWN

INDEPENDENT CONTRACTOR'S AGREEMENT

BETWEEN

....

("The company")

AND

....

("The consultant")

INTRODUCTION

The consultant has expertise and professional knowledge of .... and the company wishes to utilise his services.

The parties wish to record the basis upon which the consultant has agreed to perform the services for and on behalf of the company.

RELATIONSHIP

It is recorded that nothing in this agreement, whether express or implied, shall be construed as creating an employment relationship between the parties.

It is specifically recorded that the consultant is an independent contractor and not an employee of the company and is, as such, not entitled to any of the benefits available to the company's employees including, inter alia, medical aid, leave pay, sick leave and pension benefits.

The Consultant and where applicable its employees and agents specifically waive any right to rely on any provisions of the Labour Relations Act 66 of 1995 (as amended), the Basic Conditions of Employment Act 75 of 1997 (as amended) and the Employment Equity Act 55 of 1998 ("the Acts") and confirm that in waiving such rights to rely upon the provisions of the Acts, they do so in the full and express knowledge that they are aware of the definitions of and presumptions in favour of employee appearing in each of the Acts, and each of the consultant and, where applicable his employees and agents are not employees as defined in any of the Acts.

DURATION

With effect from .... this agreement replaced and supersedes any other agreement currently in force between the consultant and the company.

Unless terminated earlier in accordance with the termination provisions of the agreement, this agreement shall commence on .... and shall remain in force for a period of .... terminating automatically on ....

Either party may terminate the agreement by giving 30 days prior written notice.

Renewal of the contract shall be subject to the specific needs of the company and is subject to being agreed upon by the parties in writing.

Services to be provided by the consultant and performance of the services

In the performance of his duties under this agreement the consultant shall:

Well and faithfully perform the services required of him by the company;

Perform the following professional services for the benefit of the company:

....

....

The consultant will be required to submit progress reports;

The consultant shall use his own tools of trade when rendering services;

[Insert other obligations]

CONSULTANT'S FEES

In consideration for the services rendered by the consultant the company shall pay the consultant a consultancy fee of R........................, payable monthly within 30 days of receipt by the company of the consultant's invoice.

TAX

The contractor shall comply with all the provisions of the Income Tax Act, 1962, as amended, and furthermore undertakes to register as a provisional taxpayer and to obtain a certificate from the Commissioner for Inland Revenue exempting him from employees' tax.

The contractor undertakes to pay income tax, if any, directly as an independent contractor.

The contractor undertakes to provide the company with a copy of the exemption certificate received from the Commissioner for Inland Revenue prior to its undertakings in terms of this agreement.

EXPENSES

Provided that the consultant has provided the company with reasonable proof of the expenses incurred (such expenses to be confined to those specified by the company in the attached schedule marked appendix A), any expenses reasonably incurred by the consultant in the proper provision of his services in terms of the agreement in accordance with the company's scale of permissible expenses shall be for the company's account. The company shall disclose to the necessary authorities as required by law any such reimbursements or fees paid to the consultant.

CONSULTANT'S GENERAL OBLIGATIONS

The consultant shall refrain from any activities which are illegal or unethical.

The consultant shall furthermore reserve all applicable laws, ordinances, decrees, rules and regulations and service standards relating in any manner to the performance by the consultant of the obligations in terms of this agreement.

He shall also keep and maintain all records and documents which the company may reasonably require him to keep in the performance of the services in terms of the agreement.

While visiting or working at the company's facilities, the consultant shall comply with all such facility rules and regulations applicable to visitors, including in particular those relating to security and entry into and departure from such facilities.

AUTHORITY

The consultant shall not have any authority to act for or in the name of the company and he shall refrain from any representation which might lead another party to believe that he is an employee of the company.

The consultant shall further not have the authority to incur any debt or other liability or to obtain any credit facilities either in the name of or on behalf of the company without having obtained the prior written authority of the company.

ASSIGNMENT

The consultant recognises that neither this agreement nor any right or obligation of the consultant there-under may be ceded, assigned, transferred, alienated or sub-contracted by him to a third party without the prior written consent of the company.

CONFIDENTIALITY

During the duration of this agreement and subsequent thereto, the consultant shall keep confidential, shall not make use of, whether directly or indirectly, and shall not disclose any of the business, technical, tactical or financial information which he may receive from the company, or those of its subsidiaries or associate companies, or those of other persons who have made disclosures to the company under conditions of confidentiality, other than to persons authorised by the company or those employed by the company who are required to know such secrets or to have such information for the purpose of their employment or relationship with the company.

Should the consultant be uncertain as to whether any information is confidential or a trade secret, the consultant shall in writing request a ruling from the company. The consultant shall abide by any such ruling made by the company.

These confidentiality obligations shall survive the termination of this agreement and the consultant shall at no time disclose any such information to an unauthorised party.

Notwithstanding the afore-going, information received by the consultant which is or becomes available to the public without breach of this agreement, is released in writing by the company, is lawfully obtained by the consultant from a third party not obligated under a confidentiality agreement and without confidential limitation, is known to the consultant prior to the disclosure or is at any time developed by the consultant independently of any disclosure from the company shall not be construed as confidential information.

TERMINATION

The company will be entitled to terminate this agreement immediately and without notice should any of the following events arise:

The consultant is placed under judicial management or curatorship or is sequestrated or dies or becomes subject to any other legal disability;

the consultant has any judgment taken against him and fails to satisfy the judgment within 10 days of notice thereof or to rescind the judgement within the period of time prescribed in the relevant rules of court;

the consultant falsifies any documents or records required by the company or commits any act of fraud or dishonesty in respect of its dealings with the company or matters arising from the terms of this agreement;

Any attachment is levied in respect of any property or assets of the consultant pursuant to a final judgement;

The consultant fails to meet or comply with the company's standards and regulations;

The consultant commits a serious or persistent breach of any of the provisions of the agreement;

The consultant is guilty of any mismanagement or wilful neglect in the discharge of any of the obligations owed by the contractor to the company; or

the consultant commits any act that, in the reasonable opinion of the company, adversely affects or is likely to affect the goodwill and/or the reputation of the company, its subsidiaries and/or any of the employees, clients or contractors of the company.

The company's right to terminate this agreement may be exercised in addition to any other rights which the company may have against the contractor, whether in terms of this agreement or in law.

MISCELLANEOUS MATTERS

ADDRESSES

For the purposes of this agreement, including the giving of notices and the serving of legal process, the parties select domicilium citandi et executandi at the addresses recorded below:

FOR THE COMPANY:

[Insert – physical address, postal address and telefax];

FOR THE CONSULTANT:

[Insert – physical address, postal address and telefax];

The above addresses may be changed by either party on 7 days written notice to the other; provided that such address is within the Republic of South Africa. The other party shall acknowledge in writing receipt of such notice.

ARBITRATION

If any dispute arises between the parties on any matter provided for or arising directly out of this agreement or in regard to the interpretation or termination thereof, then that dispute shall be submitted to and decided by arbitration.

The dispute shall be referred to a single arbitrator to be agreed upon between the parties or, failing such agreement within 28 days after the dispute has arisen, nominated on the application of either party by the Arbitration Foundation of South Africa ("AFSA"), and any such reference shall be deemed to be a submission to the arbitration of a single arbitrator in terms of the Arbitration Act, number 42 of 1965, as amended, or any legislation passed in substitution therefore.

The award of the arbitrator shall be final and binding upon the parties.

GENERAL

No indulgence granted by a party shall constitute a waiver of any of that party's rights under this agreement. Accordingly, that party shall not be precluded as a consequence of having granted such indulgence, from exercising any rights against the other which may have arisen in the past or which may arise in the future.

No agreement varying, adding to, deleting from or cancelling this agreement shall be effective unless reduced to writing and signed by or on behalf of the parties.

This agreement contains the entire agreement between the parties and neither party shall be bound by any undertaking, representations or warranties not recorded herein or in the annexures to this agreement.

Dated at this .... day of 2020

Witness:.........................   ....

for the company

Dated at this .... day of 2020

Witness::.........................   ....

for the consultant

"Courage and perseverance have a magical talisman, before which difficulties disappear and obstacles vanish into thin air."

– JOHN QUINCY ADAMS

DON'T EVER SELL OVER EMAIL

"Luck is what happens when preparation meets opportunity."

– UNKNOWN

Now day's technology takes away the human contact – Conversations establish what the client needs.

A prospective client sends you an email requesting information about your services. You have the information they need, and you want to send it to them as quickly as possible!

You might want to believe that your responsiveness is going to make you appear professional and helpful. You might even suffer from the delusion that sending the information will help create a preference for you, your business, and your solution.

Unfortunately, the opposite is true!

When a client emails you to request information and you send it, you have allowed the client to determine that you are going to transact.

That makes you and your business transactional.

The information that you transmit isn't going to differentiate you.

If it is about your product, services, or solution, then you are not going to look a whole different from your competitors.

If it is about your services, it will generate no interest at all. If it is an answer to a question, it is unlikely to be all that different from anyone else's.

You need to create the kind of value that positions you to win. Being subservient and transactional does neither.

CONTROL THE PROCESS

When a prospective client emails you, you should pick up the phone and call them.

You don't have to agree to a transactional process – especially if you are not an undifferentiated commodity.

The questions you ask during a telephone call will do more to position you to win a new client than any information you might provide.

Asking for a meeting and sitting down face-to-face to assist your client determines what they want and need and how to get it is more powerful than to sell yourself by email.

Email isn't a good medium for selling yourself. The asynchronous nature of the communication is a poor substitute for a face-to-face meeting, a video conference, or a phone call.

If you are going to sell your services, pick up the telephone, and do everything in your power to serve your client.

AND, do everything in your power to win.

CHAPTER 25

"Life is indeed a constant cycle of rediscovery in which man sheds his relative ignorance of the past."

– A.C. FEURER

MENTORING

Mentoring is an integral part of the paralegal profession. A mentor can provide you with the necessary support, guidance and insight that your family, friends and staff may not be able to offer while you open and build your paralegal business. Whether for a short or long term relationship, a mentor may offer you advice on;

- specific or complex legal procedures

- strategy or tactical issues

- ethics and professional responsibilities

- business or practice management issues

- career and professional development

- health and wellness issues

The right mentor can assist you with the provision of legal services and may also help to reduce potential claims or complaints. The benefits of a relationship with a mentor can be immediate and enduring, and any paralegal opening a paralegal services practice should consider connecting with a mentor.

- Determine what assistance you would like from a mentor

- Consider that multiple needs may require more than one mentor

Consider sources of prospective mentors, including – community or volunteer associations (e.g. justice programs or initiatives)

- Associates based on area of law

- Associates based on demographics

- Evaluate what type of mentor relationship will best suit your need/s, considering formal and informal arrangements that may span a particular –

    » Substantive or procedural inquiry

    » Matter or file

    » Area of law

- Consider initially meeting with a prospective mentor in person to ensure that your respective personalities and mentoring styles are compatible.

- When establishing a mentor relationship, set boundaries by discussing –

    » The scope of the relationship

    » The goals or expectations of the relationship

    » How to deal with confidential information

    » How to avoid conflict of interest

    » Methods of interaction and communication

» The time available for the relationship

» How to deal with obstacles and problems

» When to evaluate the relationship

» How to provide feedback about the relationship

» When and how the relationship will end

When participating in a mentor relationship ensure that:

- You independently verify any advice, suggestions or recommendations offered to you

- Your mentor does not communicate with your clients in any way that might form a paralegal client or lawyer – client relationship

- Recognise that a mentor relationship may evolve or become obsolete

- Consider outlining the terms of your mentoring relationship in a written agreement

- Formalising your relationship may reduce your mentor's professional liability concerns

"Excellence can be attained if you care more than others think is wise, risk more than others think is safe, dream more than others think is practical and expect more than others think is possible."

– UNKNOWN

MARKETING YOUR PRACTICE

Marketing is a means to publicise your paralegal services practice, to attract and obtain the clients you want so that you may provide them the services you offer. You should complete a market research to assess the viability of your business in the market you have chosen to serve. This information is especially important to start your paralegal practice.

To develop an effective marketing plan you should first identify your target client, and the services you wish to offer. Your marketing plan should be tailored to your practice and should allow you to gain exposure to your target market at the start and throughout the evolution of your business.

Marketing includes –

- Firm name

- Signage, business cards and logo's

- Letterhead (both paper and electronic versions)

- Pamphlets and announcement cards (both paper and electronic versions)

- Website and other internet advertisements

- Consider designing and obtaining business cards as a first step, which can be used while you devise your marketing plan

- Consider the available means to market your practice to your target client, including:

  » Enrolment in a paralegal or legal services referral system

  » Advertising in a directory, in print or electronic form

  » Direct marketing via pamphlets, leaflets, mail, facsimile or e-mail

  » Networking by participation in civic or community events, local business or trade fairs or speaking engagements

Ensure that the marketing means you select to offer and market your services comply with the requirements:

- Your marketing must be demonstrably

  » True

  » Accurate

  » Identifiable

  » And does not amount to coercion, duress and harassment

- Where you use technology to market your services, ensure it is used in a manner that meets your professional obligations

- Consider the suitability of marketing methods available to your business and services and whether they will reach and attract your target market

Prepare a marketing plan that includes a description of:

- The type of client who is likely to use your services

- The potential size of the target market in your geographical area

- Your direct or indirect competition

- The major trends presently affecting your marketplace

- What makes your services unique?

- Your pricing strategy

- How you will offer your services

- How you will communicate and promote your services to your target market

*"To possess ideas is to gather flowers;
to think is to weave them in garlands."*

– GREEK PROVERB

THE ADVANTAGE OF A HUNTER CULTURE

Research has shown that the fastest growing businesses use cold calling as one of their primary methods of looking for new clients.

Small to medium size businesses benefit from building and maintaining a hunter culture.

Growth is found through the continuous creation of opportunities, and the velocity of that growth is determined by the ability to create and capitalise on opportunities.

As your business grows, there is a place for new tools and new processes. But, that doesn't require that you replace a hunter culture or the activities that build opportunities.

Cold calling has fallen out of fashion, and with it the accountability for the business owner to generate leads.

A business owner that has a hunter culture produces more opportunities and growth through opportunity creation.

CHAPTER 28

"Discipline is the bridge between goals and accomplishments."

– JIM ROHN

SPECIAL POWER OF ATTORNEY

DEFINITION: SPECIAL POWER OF ATTORNEY

A special power of attorney, also called a limited power of attorney, grants an agent (also called an attorney-in-fact). The authority to act on behalf of the principle (the person granting to act on behalf of the principle (the person granting this authority) under certain, specified circumstances.

Before you take on any work to assist a client make sure they sign a SPECIFIC POWER OF ATTORNEY giving you permission to assist them. This document is the most important part of being a successful paralegal. It must clearly state what the Specific Power of Attorney is for and what work must be undertaken in the form of assisting. I have drawn up a specimen for your perusal.

SPECIAL POWER OF ATTORNEY

I, the undersigned,

(...................................)

Identity Number

(...................................)_

Do hereby nominate, constitute and appoint (..........................)
Identity Number (..........................) as my duly authorised
agent to act on my behalf in my name and attend to all
matters relating to............................. To assist, negotiate and
mediate on my behalf.

Given under my hand at (.......................) this (............) day of
(..................) (............)

SIGNED: (full signature) (print names in full)

Without this document I really would recommend that you
do not undertake any paralegal work. If you do you are
opening up a can of worms for yourself by implicating yourself to be an attorney. I personally will never assist a client
without one.

CHAPTER 29

"The only journey is the one within."

– RAINER MARIA RILKE

MANDATES

DEFINITION

Noun;

1. An official order or commission to do something

2. The authority to carry out a policy, regarded as given by the electorate to a party or candidate that wins an election

Verb;

1. Give (someone) authority to act in a certain way

Included in the Power of Attorney I also ask for a mandate from the client requesting that they record the exact details of the work they need assistance with. With this document I then discuss with them the work I am allowed to undertake and what work has to be done by an attorney. At no point must the client be led to believe that you can take care of the complete mandate. Again, I must stress that you should take the mandate to the attorney and discuss exactly what is expected by all parties.

As far as paralegal fee's go, I am not at liberty nor legally allowed to discuss what consultation fee you must charge for your services as a paralegal assisting with paperwork. This point is entirely your choice and I would suggest that you speak to the attorney that you are working through for advice.

CHAPTER 30

*"Achieving one's goal is worth the candle
that may have to burn late into the night, the
rewards more than justify the efforts."*

– UNKNOWN

ASSISTING THE COURTS

I have mentioned in a previous chapter that the best training a paralegal will benefit from is offering your services (pro-bono) at the courts assisting people to fill in documents correctly. That way you will become a specialist in the various courts when it comes to court procedures and court applications. This advice is worth at least 2 years income and of course the respect of clerks of the court.

By offering this service at the courts you are assisting the court, the clerk of the court and the magistrates.

Many people spend hours in the queue waiting to see the relevant court official only to be handed a form to fill in and then have to return with the documents filled in, only to join the queue again.

Many hours are spent in these queue's wasting time for all parties, hence many woman just give up on the maintenance claim they so need and deserve or they give up on that assault and battery case, human rights violations etc etc.

By assisting the courts you are also assisting the very people who need help the most. I personally spent many hours assisting the courts and people with this and have found myself feeling such gratitude and fulfilment at the end of the day.

Not only did I learn so much, but my people skills developed along the way.

The gratitude shown by the people you assist is enormous as they feel so lost and always remember that the court is their last resort for assistance.

CHAPTER 31

"Mastery is the path of patient dedicated effort without attachment to immediate results."

– UNKNOWN

ASSISTING THE MAGISTRATE

Should you also be a certified mediator which I will cover in more depth in a later chapter assisting the magistrate with certain work will certainly be in your favour and the future of your consultancy business.

The magistrates in our country are more than willing to share their knowledge and remember they are there for a reason!

Get to make sure that the magistrate is aware of your services and the way to do that is through the clerk of the court.

Once the clerk trusts your work they will most certainly mention your name to the magistrate of their court who will in turn after some time test your knowledge and work ethics. So, make sure you are up to speed with the latest rulings and learn to understand how that specific magistrate likes things done.

CHAPTER 32

"We are all faced with a series of great opportunities brilliantly disguised as unsolvable problems."

– JOHN W. GARDENER

REPORTS AND LETTER WRITING

Any reports or letter writing will be a reflection of your level of professionalism in the eyes of the attorney you assist or any court official. Keep your reports to the point and stick to pertinent information. Court officials or attorneys don't have time to thrash through waffle and useless information as they are busy people.

PLANNING A REPORT

Whenever you write a report remember to follow certain planning steps

ASK YOURSELF THE FOLLOWING?

- Who am I writing for

- What do I want to tell them

- Why should they know this

- List the things you want to say

- Plan the order in which you will structure your report

- Write the report

CHAPTER 33

"You were given this life because you were strong enough to live it."

– UNKNOWN

LEARNING BY ASSISTING QUALIFIED ATTORNEYS

This is an area that I must over emphasize on. There is no university, college or school that can prepare you for the legal world than actually working for an attorney or law firm.

My recommendation is that you join up with an attorney or law firm as soon as possible if not sooner. Offer your services for free to prove yourself, offer to do handle paperwork, run errands, deliver documents to the courts all in return for knowledge.

Once you have achieved this then use the same attorney or law firm for your consultancy business.

EARN WHILE YOU LEARN

Always remember that an attorney cannot share his fees with you, but, you are allowed to charge a fee for services directly to the client before you hand the file over to the attorney.

CHAPTER 34

'If you close your eyes to facts, you will learn through accidents."

– AFRICAN PROVERB

LEGAL AID SOUTH AFRICA

WHO QUALIFIES FOR LEGAL AID?

Legal Aid South Africa has a mandate from the South African Constitution to help the poor get taxed-funded legal assistance.

If you approach Legal Aid for assistance they will ask you to complete a form so that they can understand how much money you get each month and what assets you own, like a car or house. This is called a Means Test.

LEGAL AID FOR INDIVIDUALS

If you are employed, you must earn less than R5500.00 per month after tax has been deducted

LEGAL AID FOR HOUSEHOLDS

If you live with other people for more than four nights per week and these other people share in the cost of food and other costs, then Legal Aid will look at your total household income. They will only give legal aid to households that earn less than R6000.00 per month. Again, they will only look at the amount that the household receives after tax has been taken off

Legal Aid also takes into account what you own:

- If you or your household

- Own a home, then the total value of the home and all your belongings must not be worth more than R500 000.00

- You must also only have one house and you must live in it

- Do not own a house? Then the total value of all your belongings (for example, your car, furniture, clothes and other personal things) must not be worth more than R100 000.00

- Some people automatically qualify for legal aid

- People on a State Grants and the elderly

  » If you receive any state grants or old age pension, you automatically qualify for legal aid. You do not have to take the Means Test. You will need to show them official documents that prove you receive a state grant or pension

CHILDREN

In criminal cases, children automatically qualify for legal aid and do not have to take the Means Test. If it is a civil case, the family of the child will need to take and pass the Means Test.

LEGAL AID FOR NON-CITIZENS

- Legal aid is available to anyone who lives in South Africa (not only South African citizens) if the case

- Is criminal

- Involves children

- Asylum seekers – Legal aid is available to Asylum seekers applying or intending to apply for asylum under Chapters 3 and 4 of the Refugees Act 130 of 1998

- In civil cases legal aid is not available to non-citizens

YOU DON'T PAY FOR LEGAL AID

If you qualify for legal aid, and they have agreed to represent you, you will not have to pay for any services. In fact, Legal Aid South Africa lawyers may not request fee's or be paid any remuneration when they assist you with your case

LEGAL AID SOUTH AFRICA MAY DEDUCT COSTS AND BENEFITS

Although you don't pay for legal aid, if you should win a civil case they will deduct the money that the court grants to pay for costs and benefits, before they pay the money owing to you

LEGAL AID SOUTH AFRICA ALSO CONSIDERS SPECIAL LEGAL CASES

Legal Aid South Africa tries to assist as many people who can't afford help as possible. From time to time, opportunities arise for them to take on legal work that has the potential to positively change lives of a far larger number of people than just the person that they provide legal assistance to. These cases fall under their Impact Litigation Programme.

(www.legal-aid.co.za)

CHAPTER 35

"The only way of discovering the limits of the possible is to venture a little way past them into the impossible."

– ARTHUR C. CLARK

BUSINESS RESCUE

COMPANIES ACT, 2008

To provide for the incorporation, registration, organisation and management of companies, the capitalisation of private companies, and the registration of offices for foreign companies carrying on business within the Republic; to define the relationship between companies and their respective shareholders or members and directors; to provide for efficient amalgamations, mergers and takeovers of companies; to provide appropriate legal redress for investors and third parties with respect to companies; to establish a Companies and Intellectual Property Commission and a Takeover Regulation Panel to administer the requirements of the Act with respect to companies, to establish a Companies Tribunal to facilitate alternative dispute resolution and to review decisions of the Commission; to establish a Financial Reporting Standards Council to advise on requirements for financial record-keeping and reporting by companies; to repeal the Companies Act, 1973 (Act No.61 of 1973), and make amendments to the Close Corporations Act, 1984 (Act No. 69 of 1984), as necessary to provide for a consistent and harmonious regime of business incorporation and regulation; and to provide for matters connected therewith.

For Further Information (www.cipc.co.za)

In 1926 South Africa was the first country after the USA to have introduced business rescue legislation.

Judicial management however proved to be ineffective and on the 1 May 2011 was replaced with the business rescue provision in Chapter 6 of the new company legislation.

Chapter 6 business rescue legislation represents a codification of the turnaround procedures followed in workout (informal turnaround) in the informal sector, but is designed to overcome a number of practical problems faced by workout, and to protect the interests of all stakeholders. It comes with its own problems though and financially distressed companies will always have to make the choice between informal turnaround and Chapter 6 (business rescue) based on the specific circumstances they face.

That notwithstanding, new business rescue legislation implemented on the 1 May 2011 represents an important new era in the South African turnaround industry with the potential of saving many more financially distressed but economically viable companies from liquidation.

For further information (www.business-rescue.co.za)

DEFINITIONS OF CHAPTER 6 OF THE COMPANIES ACT 2008

BUSINESS RESCUE

Business rescue means the plans and steps taken to rescue and rehabilitate a company that is financially distressed by:

- Putting in place the temporary supervision of the company and the management of its affairs, business and property

- Putting a temporary moratorium in place to prevent creditors claiming against the company or any property in its possession

- Developing and implementing, if approved, a plan to rescue the company:

  » By restructuring its affairs, business properly, equity, debt and other liabilities in a manner that maximises the likely hood of the company's continued and solvent existence or,

  » If a business rescue is not possible then by developing and implementing a plan which results in the company's creditors or shareholders getting a better return than if the company was simply liquidated.

FINANCIAL DISTRESS

Financial distress for a company means that:

- It appears to be reasonably unlikely that the company will be able to pay all of its debts as they fall due and payable within the immediate ensuing 6 months (commercial insolvency)

- It appears to be reasonably likely that the company will become "insolvent" within the immediate ensuing 6 months (factual insolvency)

BUSINESS RESCUE PRACTITIONER

A business rescue practitioner is one or more persons appointed to oversee a company during a business rescue operation.

126

AFFECTED PERSON

In relation to a company an affected person is:

- A shareholder or creditor of the company in distress

- Any registered trade union representing employees of the company in distress

- If any of the employees of the distressed company are not represented by a registered trade union, each of those employees or their respective representatives

CHAPTER 36

"Take risks; if you win, you will be happy;
if you lose, you will be wise."

– UNKNOWN

MEDIATION

ATTORNEYS LITIGATE – PARALEGALS MEDIATE

WHAT IS MEDIATION?

It is a process by which a mediator assists parties in a legal dispute by:

- Facilitating discussions between parties

- Assisting them in identifying issues

- Exploring areas of compromise

- Generating options in an attempt to resolve the dispute

Mediation is an alternative to having the dispute resolved in court.

WHAT ARE THE ADVANTAGES OF MEDIATION?

- It offers speedy resolution of disputes

- It is considerably cheaper than litigation

- It provides a win-win situation for both parties in a dispute

- The process is flexible and avoids technicalities

- It is a voluntary process

- It promotes reconciliation

- Parties can use their own languages

WHICH MATTERS CAN BE REFERRED FOR MEDIATION?

Most disputes are appropriate for mediation, as long as the court has jurisdiction in respect of the matter.

ANY DISAGREEMENT BETWEEN PARTIES CAN BE MEDIATED!

The magistrate courts are currently over-flowing with cases. Various disputes are brought before the courts on a daily basis.

Attempts to get a trial date or a date on the roll can leave you waiting for months before your matter is heard. In light of the above, the legislature has looked into ways in which we can reduce the amount of cases that go to trial, in essence, alternative dispute resolution.

In December 2014, CH 2 of the magistrate's court rules came into operation providing an alternative to formal litigation, namely voluntary mediation.

Mediation is the process whereby a third party, namely a mediator, assists the parties in identifying issues, clarifying priorities, exploring areas of compromise and generating options in an attempt to resolve that dispute.

The mediation process is to facilitate discussion between parties.

A matter can be referred to mediation before or after litigation but must be done before judgment is handed down.

If the trial has commenced the parties must first obtain consent from the court to proceed with mediation.

Parties desiring to refer the matter mediation, both prior to the commencement of litigation and during the commencement of litigation, must make a request in writing to the clerk of the court.

The clerk of the court must inform all parties to the dispute that mediation is being sought and must call on all the parties to attend a conference within ten days for the purpose of determining whether all or some of the parties agree to refer the dispute to mediation.

In the event that litigation has already commenced the parties are to provide the mediator with copies of the summons and plea, or statement of defence where no plea is filed in the case of action proceedings.

In application proceedings the parties are to lodge copies of the founding, answering and replying affidavits or statement of defence if no answering affidavit has been filed.

The parties are entitled to file, with the clerk of the court any document or evidential material on which the action is based, or which the parties intend to use at mediation proceedings at least seven days before the mediation proceedings. The parties may also file or supplement these documents during the mediation proceedings.

The parties have a right to be represented at mediation proceedings; however, this is not mandatory. (I quite frankly do not agree to this as attorneys have a very different view point to mediation unless they have been trained to understand the mediation process). Always remember that an attorney is there to litigate.

Should parties reach an agreement as a result of the mediation, the mediator must assist the parties to draft the settlement agreement, which must then be transmitted by the mediator to the clerk.

On receipt of the agreement the clerk must place the agreement before a magistrate in chambers for noting that the dispute has been resolved or to make the agreement an order of court, by the agreement of the parties.

If settlement is not reached in mediation between parties, the clerk must, on receipt of the report from the mediator, file the report to enable litigation to continue, from which all suspended time periods will continue to run.

Mediation is quicker than the usual route of full blown litigation and is more cost effective, amicable and may prove more successful for both parties involved.

Attorneys, litigants and parties to a dispute are encouraged to entertain the mediation route and settle their disputes cordially outside court.

Credit – Caitlin Asken LLB (Rhodes) BKM Attorneys

ALTERNATIVE DISPUTE RESOLUTION IS THE WAY FORWARD FOR PARALEGALS TO MAKE A DIFFERENCE

RULE 41A

Rules Board For Courts of Law – Republic of South Africa.

Proposed Uniform Rule 41A: Mediation As A Dispute Mechanism.

The Rules Board for Courts of Law (Rules Board) intends introducing into the Uniform Rules, a rule to regulate the procedure for referral to mediation of cases in the High Court.

The proposed new Rule is intended to be numbered and named: '41A Mediation as a Dispute Resolution Mechanism'.

Unlike the Chapter 2 rules of the Magistrates' Courts, the mediation contemplated for cases in the High Court is not intended to be court-annexed. The proposed new rule is intended to facilitate mediation contemplated by the parties or recommended by the court and to provide the procedure for referral to mediation in terms of Rule 37(6)(d) (Pre-trial Conference) and Rule 37(10) (Judicial Case Management).

The Main Features of Proposed New Rule 41A are:

a.) To require the parties, when issuing summons or application or delivering a plea or answering affidavits, to indicate whether they consider mediation to be possible or not and to give reasons for either consideration;

b.) The parties are to deliver a joint minute recording their agreement to refer the dispute to mediation;

c.) The suspension of time limits to deliver pleadings whilst mediation is in progress;

d.) The procedure where multiple parties are involved in the litigation and some parties proceed to mediation, whilst others do not;

e.) The admissibility and confidentiality of documents;

f.) A joint minute indicating the outcome of mediation proceedings; and

g.) Costs of the mediation proceedings and costs orders.

The proposed Rule does not contemplate provision for pre-litigation mediation, since mediation is not court-annexed.

41A – Mediation as a dispute resolution mechanism.

1. In this Rule –

"dispute" means the subject matter of litigation between parties, or an aspect thereof, including litigation which is about to be commenced;

"mediation" means (1) the process by which a neutral and independent person, the mediator, assists the parties to resolve the dispute between them by facilitating discussions between parties, assisting them in identifying issues, clarifying priorities, exploring areas of compromise and generating options to resolve the dispute.

"mediation" means (2) the process by which an impartial third party (the mediator) will facilitate communication between the parties and assist them in their negotiation as they attempt to reach an agreed settlement of their dispute.

"mediator" means (1) a person who has undergone training and who is certified competent to conduct mediation.

"mediator" means (2) a person who in the opinion of the parties is (sufficiently skilled and) competent to conduct mediation.

2.

    a.) In every new action or application commenced, the plaintiff or applicant shall, together with the summons or notice of motion, deliver a notice indicating whether such plaintiff or applicant agrees to or opposes referral of the dispute to mediation;

    b.) A defendant or respondent shall, when delivering a plea or answering affidavit, deliver a notice indicating whether such defendant or respondent agrees to or opposes referral of the dispute to mediation;

    c.) The notice referred to in sub-rules (a) and (b) shall be as clearly as possible in accordance with the 'Notice Agreement or Opposition to Mediation' and shall clearly and concisely indicate the reasons for such party's belief that the dispute is or is not capable of being mediated;

    d.) Subject to the provisions of sub-rule 9 (c) the notice referred to in this sub-rule shall be of a "Without Prejudice" nature and shall not form part of the record of the trial or hearing.

3.

a.) The parties may at any stage before judgment, agree to refer the dispute between them to mediation: Provided that where the trial or opposed application has commenced the parties must obtain the leave of the Court;

b.) A Judge, or a Case Management Judge referred to in Rule 37A or the Court may at any stage before judgment direct the parties to consider referral of a dispute to mediation, whereupon the parties may agree to refer the dispute or any aspect thereof to mediation;

c.) Any issue of fact which is in dispute, the mediation of which may not necessarily result in settlement but which may result in the curtailment of the issues, may be referred to mediation, as provided in this sub-rule.

4. Where a dispute or any aspect thereof is referred to mediation –

a.) The parties shall deliver a joint signed minute recording their election to refer the dispute or any portion thereof to mediation;

b.) The parties shall prior to the commencement of mediation proceedings enter into an agreement to mediate, which shall be as closely as possible in accordance with 'Notice of Agreement or Opposition to Mediation'.

c.) The time limits prescribed for the delivery of pleadings and notices and the filing of affidavits or the taking of any step shall be suspended for every party from the date of signature of the minute referred to in sub-rule (a) to the time of conclusion of mediation;

and

d.) Mediation shall be concluded within 30 days from
the date of signature of the minute referred to in sub-
rule (a) : Provided that a Judge or the court may on
good cause shown by the parties extend such time
period for the completion of the meditation session.

5.

a.) In proceedings where there are multiple parties some
of whom are agreeable to mediation and some of
whom are not, parties who are agreeable to mediation may proceed to mediation notwithstanding any
other party's refusal to mediate;

b.) The time limits prescribed for the delivery of pleadings and notices and the filing of affidavits or the
taking of any step shall be suspended for every party
from the date of signature of the minute referred to in
sub-rule (4)(a) to the time of conclusion of mediation
by the parties who have elected to mediate;

c.) In any matter where there are multiple issues, the
parties may agree that some issues remaining in dispute may proceed to litigation;

d.) If any issue remains in dispute after mediation, the
parties may proceed to litigation on such issue in dispute;

6. Except as provided by law, or discoverable in terms of
the rules or agreed between parties, all communications and disclosures, whether oral or written, made
at mediation proceedings shall be confidential and
inadmissible in evidence.

7.

    a.) Upon conclusion of mediation the parties who engaged in mediation shall inform the registrar and all other parties by notice that mediation has been completed;

    b.) Notwithstanding the failure of parties who have engaged in mediation to deliver the notice referred to in sub-rule (a), the suspension of the time limits referred to in sub-rule (4)(c) shall lapse unless a Judge or a Court has extended the time limit and notice thereof has been given to all parties to the proceedings within 5 days of such order.

8.

    a.) The parties who engaged in mediation and the mediator who conducted the mediation shall issue a joint minute indicating –

    i) Whether full or partial settlement was reached or whether mediation was successful; and

    ii) The issues upon which agreement was reached and which do not require hearing by the court;

    b.) It shall be the joint responsibility of the parties who engaged in mediation to file with the registrar, the minute referred to in sub-rule(a);

    c.) Where the parties have reached settlement at mediation proceedings the provisions of Rule 41A shall apply *mutatis mutandis.*

9.

    a.)   The parties may agree amongst them how the costs of the mediation proceedings are to be borne: Provided that any party may, prior to an agreement to mediate, offer or undertake to pay the mediation costs in full or the portion due by any party;

    b.)   The court may, at the trial or hearing of a matter which has been referred to mediation and where the parties have not been able to reach agreement on the liability for the costs of the mediation proceedings, make an appropriate order of such costs;

    c.)   In considering an appropriate order for costs the court may have regard to the notices referred to in sub-rule(2) and any party shall be entitled to bring such notices to the attention of the Court.

www.justice.gov.za

I am pleased to say that the Rule 41A came into operation on the 9th March 2020. Once again it shows how mediation and the legal system for practitioners and consultants is changing in leaps and bounds.

There is no better time than now to study further in the field of mediation and human behaviour.

CHAPTER 37

WHAT IS NEGOTIATION?

"It's a discussion between two parties trying to reach a common agreement to solve a problem"

In the negotiation process two or more parties come together to negotiate on how to reach an agreement on the problem and if there is a problem in reaching the agreement a MEDIATOR is called to intervene.

THE NEGOTIATION SKILLS

The skills in the negotiation process are very important as two or more parties have different agendas and they must try and work towards reaching a goal which will benefit all parties.

STEPS IN THE NEGOTIATION PROCESS

All parties should acknowledge that they have a problem and should see the need in solving it through negotiation.

The parties should contribute towards what they feel should be a solution to the problem and they must try and speak through the issues, working on what they want to achieve in the process.

Then the parties should agree on working together to solve the problem.

Strategies that could be used in negotiation

- In most cases negotiators ask for information from experts or do research regarding the issue to be negotiated.

- Negotiators use strategies to support arguments and supporting information to convince the other party regarding the issue negotiated

- Power negotiation is the ability to affect the other party's decision therefore it is advisable for a paralegal to start his negotiation with extreme position – by letting the other party know that you are in charge by talking with confidence

- The negotiator who knows the interest of the people can negotiate and influence parties to make decisions that are suitable for all parties concerned.

- Cultural differences can also be a huge impact in the negotiation process between parties, therefore it is important to understand other people and their culture.

- A good working relationship can also influence power in a negotiator resulting in the other party's having trust and agreeing to one goal.

CHAPTER 38

"We need to be the change we wish to see in the world."

– MAHATMA GHANDI

SECTORS OF LAW TO CONSIDER AS A PARALEGAL.

FAMILY LAW

This area of the law is very exciting, fulfilling and draining all at the same time.

So many families are in need of advice, direction and in need of someone who actually cares about the family and children.

Many divorces, family disputes and maintenance disagreements can be sorted out amicably by the right paralegal.

I again remind you as a paralegal that most attorneys are there to litigate and paralegals are there to resolute. It is a trying time for the parents and children who often feel that they may be cause of the problems arising from the divorce or family dispute.

It is up to us the paralegals to set the pace before handing over to an attorney.

DISPUTE RESOLUTION IS CRUCIAL

Family conflicts are a natural phenomenon.

Disputes within the family are a part of the basic human lifestyle and creates a process of gaining better understanding to the evolution of human relationships.

There are innumerable options to evaluate and resolve family conflicts as counselling, facilitation, litigation, psycho-therapy, arbitration, and most importantly mediation.

Mediation is a path of love and compassion that offers a win-win ideal process in allowing the family conflict to a natural, harmonious resolution.

There are 10 reasons listed below why mediation creates such a holistic and balanced approach in generating more love within family conflicts.

1. **Lack of Stresses and Pressure**

    The process of mediation is completely voluntary for all parties involved including the mutual mediator. Spouses can terminate the process whenever they want but no one can impose any type of decisions upon them.

    Unlike litigation or arbitration that may host a win-lose ideal with limited options, mediation opens creative doorways to infinite opportunities for all parties involved in setting a win-win ideal standard and allowing the parties to be empowered within to come to a mutual agreement or resolution (Grusin, 2015).

    In the engagement of mediation, parties often stand alone with mediators, and in the absence of the other party, they can divulge about all of their desires, problems, and perspectives, while the neutral mediator empowers them to discover creative and holistic options in the process.

2. **Equanimity and Emotional Balance**

One of the major affairs dealing with family conflicts is substantial emotional pain for all parties involved in the conflict. In most cases, spouses usually dramatize the controversies and often consider harming one another as the only option. Mediation recognizes emotions from an equitable stance, transcends the orthodox win-lose models (especially litigation), and offers a holistic process for all parties to express themselves in a healthy manner (Malcolm and O'Donnell, 2009).

It is aimed to help parties seek a resolution that will meet their interests in a strictly confidential extrajudicial procedure that is also intertwined with a humanistic extensive empathy, love compassion by the neutral mediator.

3. **Emergence of Loyalty and Trust**

Another essential element of a mediator's influence on the restoration of healthy family relationships is loyalty and trust, which has two aspects. Firstly, each spouse knows that his/her partner always works with the best prompts. Secondly, each spouse is sure that his/her partner will never hurt intentionally (Nolan, 2013). This is the holistic foundation of mutual principles for the benefit of the whole family.

4. **Induction of Kindness and Benevolence**

Usually, the emotions of the parties in breaking the marriage are an obstacle to a civilized settlement of all the necessary moments of further life. When, spouses come to the mediator with a firm decision to separate or dealings of child custody for example, it is advisable to consult such clients about key issues. In such situations, reconciliation is likely to happen (Beardsley, 2011). Thus, to a certain extent, the degree of hostility is reduced and the attention of the parties switches to maintaining relationships with holistic factors as kindness and benevolence.

5. Neutrality

The mediator is not allowed to support one of the parties and is an impartial participant in all conflict discussions. Furthermore, the mediator also provides restoration of the ability to negotiate with the partners in the conflict, structures of the conflict, and organizes the negotiation situation for the benefit of all parties involved (Ashley, 2001). The neutral mediator helps parties develop a holistic, mutually acceptable, and viable resolution process in the context of their existing divergent interests.

6. Evolution of Equal Vision

Selfish and sublime attitudes of one partner to another are common and frequent appearances in the family misalliances. The inequality of partners is of a very social nature in unbalanced family relationships (Herbert and others, 2011).

Mediation sets a strong ideal in not only avoiding the root of the problem but also aids in transcending the family conflict. The holistic standard is to seek solace, support, and re-education through the neutral mediator in discovering equality and a harmonious balance in family relationships.

7. Bona Fide Impacts

The bona fide mediator restores the ability of the spouses to exert a healthy and positive influence on each other, instead of forcing a resolution, the mediator pays particular attention to the ability to carefully listen and respond holistically with love and compassion (Roepstorff and Bernhard, 2013). The evolution of the mediation process allows each of the spouses to develop a strong conviction that he/she can fully express the feelings and will be listened to with dignity, sincerity, love, and respect.

8. Empathy

The positive difference between mediation and psychotherapy is that during mediation partners do not clarify relationships, but seek a solution with a third party (Mackinnon and Fairchild, 2009). The neutral mediator serves to engage the parties in conflict through empathy and deeper understanding. The journey of mediation is not about the change of family relations. The primary focus is about discovering the root of the family conflict. Furthermore, the solutions of which is achieved by active contributions of the conflicting parties themselves through guidance and holistic empowerment strategies of the neutral mediator.

9. Emergence of Dignity and Stature

The constitutional focus of family happiness is having a strong sense of dignity and respect for the partner and the whole family, establishing unity, without which the family foundation is destroyed (McEwen and others, 2014). The mediator teaches couples that this sincere stature is based on awareness and acceptance of both the strengths and weaknesses of the partner.

10. Visionary Model of Solving Family Conflicts for the Future

The mediator's competence includes not only the duty to help solve an already existing conflict, but also to teach the parties not to allow such situations or at least to correctly solve them in the future (Moose, 2014). Ultimately, the mediation process offers a visionary model for preventive strategies, especially in generating a harmonious flow of energy for the holistic benefit of all parties involved in a family conflict. With this training, all of the parties involved in the family conflict will fully understand the consequences of their own discussions.

Ultimately, one can say that the bona fide mediator creates holistic conditions for work and its style, maintains equanimity, loyalty, benevolence, and neutrality, seeks for dignity, equal vision, respect, empathy, and trust within the interaction of all parties involved in a family conflict.

Conflicting partners with the mediator's help represent their positions, visions, and interests from the current situation and all harmoniously develop solutions. The mediator finds a holistic, balanced, and visionary approach to conflicting sides, helps them to resolve problems, activates future prevention strategies, and this contributes to generating more love for a family conflict. (Credit- Dr Denisha Shah, 2017).

CHAPTER 39

*"There are better things ahead than
what we leave behind."*

– C. S. LEWIS

WILLS AND ESTATES

This area of law is a prime piece of real estate for a paralegal to invest time in. So many people need guidance and assistance when having to wind up an estate on behalf of a deceased whether testate or intestate.

It is during the initial stages that family members need someone to lean on and show them the way forward.

The law of succession regulates how a person's assets are to devolve after death.

The living relatives only realize how much paper work there is when they see what the formal requirements are needed to proceed as regulated by the Wills Act 7 of 1953.

This is where the paralegal's knowledge is invaluable.

By assisting the family members going forward they will also realize the importance of a valid will which opens up another opportunity for the paralegal to be service.

What I have come to realize in South Africa is that not many paralegals fully understand the stirpes calculations and the full mechanics enough to explain to surviving family members.

As much as this area of service is viable it can also be your downfall if you venture into Wills and Estates without the necessary knowledge and training.

There is nothing worse than in your moment of need you are dealing with somebody you trust and they are not qualified to fulfil their obligations.

Please respect the family and know your job or recommend a person who does.

As a paralegal make sure you making quite clear that your position is that of an agent and have the client sign a power of attorney.

You must also make it quite clear that once you have completed your obligations you will need to nominate an attorney to fulfil the rest of the procedure.

CHAPTER 40

"Strength does not come from winning. Your struggles develop your strength. When you go through hardships and decide not to surrender, that is strength."

– ARNOLD SCHWARZENEGGER

PRACTISING MINDFULNESS

"Mindfulness is the stripping down of the casual body to its naked truth."

– JOHAN CLAASSENS

Listed below are a few points which I believe contribute to the very essence of mindfulness –

- Self awareness

- Vision

- Deep understanding of yourself

- Agility

- Values

- Contribute to human welfare

- Passion

- Outcomes based

- Don't impress – be who you are

- Vulnerability – source of your power

- Focus – what's important in your life and that of others

- Clarity

- Creativity

- Power to influence people

HEART BRAIN VS HEAD BRAIN

What many people don't know is that the human heart has its own brain with neurons.

In addition to the extensive neural communication network linking the heart with the brain and body, the heart also communicates information to the brain and throughout the body via electromagnetic field interactions.

The heart generates the body's most powerful and most extensive rhythmic electromagnetic field.

If the messages sent from the heart brain are in conflict with the head brain there will be a conflict in messages throughout the neural pathways thus creating anxiety, depression etc.

So just to work with the main brain without considering the heart brain will not have a lasting effect. Mindfulness starts with love which has its starting point in the heart brain.

WHOLE BRAIN THINKING

*"If the brain were so simple we could easily understand it,
we would be so simple we couldn't."*

– LYALL WATSON (1939-2008)

Applying 'Whole Brain Thinking' means being able to fully leverage one's own preferences, stretching to other quadrants when necessary, and adapt to and take advantage of the preferences of those around you to improve performance and results.

WHAT ARE THE 4 QUADRANTS OF THE BRAIN?

The brain is divided into four quadrants-

- Analytical

- Practical

- Relational

- Experimental

The premise being that each of us prefers to think in one, or a combination of the quadrants.

ANALYTICAL

- Knows how things work

- Knows about money

- Likes numbers

- Is realistic

- Is critical

- Is logical

- Quantities

- Analyzes

PRACTICAL

- Plans

- Timely

- Is neat

- Organizes

- Is reliable

- Gets things done

- Establishes procedures

- Takes preventative action

RELATIONAL

- Feels

- Talks a lot

- Is emotional

- Is expressive

- Is supportive

- Touches a lot

- Likes to teach

- Is sensitive to others

EXPERIMENTAL

- Infers

- Imagines

- Is curious/plays

- Likes surprises

- Breaks rules

- Speculates

- Is impulsive and take risks

"Whole Brain Thinking is the awareness of one's own thinking preferences and the thinking preferences of others, combined with the ability to act outside of one's preferred thinking preferences".

– NED HERMANN

CHAPTER 41

"To rise from error to truth is rare and beautiful."

– VICTOR HUGO

EMOTIONAL BODY

There are currently two main scientific ways of explaining the nature of emotions.

According to the cognitive appraisal theory, emotions are judgments about the extent that the current situation meets your goals.

Happiness is the evaluation that your goals are being satisfied.

Others have argued that emotions are perceptions of changes in your body such as heart rate, breathing rate, perspiration, and hormone levels.

In this view, happiness is a kind of physiological perception, not a judgment, and other emotions such as sadness and anger are mental reactions to different kinds of physiological stages.

The problem with this account is that bodily states do not seem to be nearly as finely tuned as the many different kinds of emotional states. Yet, there is undoubtedly some connection between emotions and physiological changes.

Understanding how the brain works shows that these theories of emotions – cognitive appraisal and physiological perception – can be combined into a united account of emotions.

Similarly, the brain can perform emotions by interactively combining both high – level judgments about goal satisfactions and low-level perceptions of bodily changes.

(Credit – Paul Thagard, Ph.D.)

HOW TO INTERPRET BODY LANGUAGE IN A BUSINESS ENVIRONMENT

Communication is both verbal and non-verbal.

Verbal communication is spoken words, it is what we say.

Non-verbal communication is without the use of words, and normally referred to as 'body language'. This includes:

- Facial expressions

- Signs

- Body posture etc.

Body language is used to enhance verbal communication.

Good communicators are those who have mastered the art to complement what they say with the appropriate body language.

Sometimes though, our body language contradicts what we say. When somebody says they are happy with your decisions, but whilst saying this they frown, what are they actually trying to say to you? As a rule, ACTIONS SPEAK LOUDER THAN WORDS.

It is therefore important; to always be aware of your body language and that of the people you are interacting with.

Learn to look out for the following:

- Facial expressions – Are you or the person you are interacting with smiling or frowning

- Gestures – eye contact, waving of hands, shaking of fists, touching the face or pulling at the hair

- Posture – drooping shoulders, posing, tense posture

- Body space – does the client appear unwilling to face you openly?

- Colours – the use of colours in dress can reflect the mood

- Voice pitch – tempo, intensity, tone, filler sounds

- Silence – does the client appear uncomfortably during silences?

- The use of touch – this should not apply in a business environment

Listen for information in a verbal communication.

Listening is important because you make things easier for people as you reduce the misunderstandings from information provided.

While listening, you must be attentive to understand what is being said to you.

To be an effective listener you must be free and committed to listening:

- Show interest on what the speaker is saying

- Do not just listen; show the speaker interest in what he is saying by using the non verbal communication skills.

- If you have enough information/knowledge of things related to what it is that you are listening to it becomes easier for you to understand.

- Listening helps to understand the issues revolving around you and your environment and the way you should communicate as well.

- Effective listening also involves understanding the body language that the client is giving while explaining, the tone of voice, gestures and expressions on their face

- A person who listens attentively becomes a good person to handle issues as he understands what to do and what to say

- A good listener listens more to what the conversation is all about and gives inputs where necessary.

LISTENING IS CRUCIAL BECAUSE

- You gain a lot of information

- It can make or break the relationship

- It leads to better communication

TYPES OF LISTENING SKILLS

Listening can be characterized into 5 different groups:

1. INADEQUATE LISTENING

- Is listening to a person and thinking that he is saying something while he means another. Instead of listening to what the client is saying and listening with an open mind, you are destructed by your own thoughts.

2. EVALUATIVE LISTENING

- Is judging the client on what he might be saying, before he could even finish talking. As a result the listener's response is judgmental.

- In return the client will not get help as you already evaluated them without giving them the benefit of the doubt or listening to what they had to say.

3. FILTERED LISTENING

- When you use your own frame of reference and your previous experience to compare it with what the client is saying making you hear what is inappropriate.

4. CENTRED LISTENING

- Listening to what you asking for, not wanting to hear the depth of the story and therefore closing up to other possibilities.

5. SYMPATHETIC LISTENING

- When you listen with passion and put yourself in the client's shoes.

- When you feel sympathetic towards their problem.

- This results in helping the client because you understand and feel their problem.

- This is an important skill that any counsellor should acquire.

It is crucial to know exactly what to say when talking to others, as communication is the key to all relationships, both business and personal.

Make sure that what you say is understandable, clear and straight forward.

CHAPTER 42

"Failure is the only opportunity to begin again more intelligently."

– HENRY FORD

CIVIL LAW

Many civil cases can be addressed if there are willing parties.

Most of the banks, finance houses, retail stores etc are more than willing to meet halfway before applying to the courts for remedy.

Many civil cases between parties involving finances can most definitely be mediated.

I personally have yet to come across a civil matter that can't be settled out of court.

The main reason for non settlement is ego! A win at all cost mentality will cost money.

DEBT COLLECTING

This is an area that probably will fit the accounting type paralegal as the paper work is endless and certainly takes a special kind of person.

You need to be completely versed in law to undertake this mammoth task.

CHAPTER 43

"Think as if your every thought were to be etched
in fire upon the sky for all to and everything to see,
for so in truth it is ......"

– BOOK OF MIRDAD

NATIONAL CREDIT REGULATOR (NCR)

THE NATIONAL CREDIT ACT, 2005 (ACT NO.34 OF 2005)

The NCR promotes a fair and non-discriminatory market place for access of consumer credit and provide for the general regulation of consumer credit and improved standards of consumer information, promotes black economic empowerment and ownership within the consumer credit industry and prohibits certain unfair credit and credit marketing practices, promotes responsible credit granting and use, and for that purpose to prohibit reckless credit granting, provides for debt re-organisation in cases of over indebtedness, regulates credit bureaus, credit providers and debt counselling services, establishes national norms and standards relating to consumer credit, promotes a consistent enforcement framework relating to consumer credit.

The Usury Act was the primary legislation that regulated the industry. This Act was, generally, intended to regulate the cost of credit and to ensure that there were proper disclosures in credit agreements.

It applied to money lending transactions (mainly from R10 0000.00 to R500 000.00), credit transactions and leasing transactions (movable properties).

The Usury Act was, generally, critized for being too complicated and difficult to comprehend.

Towards 1992 government realised that the Usury Act and its stringent limitations on the cost of credit had, unfortunately, contributed to inadequate access to credit for the majority of the population of the country.

In order to promote more access, they introduced, in 1992, the first Exemption Notice to the Usury Act (GN 3451 OF 31 December 1992) which exempted all loans that were below R6000.00 from the Act.

Another important piece of legislation that regulated the credit industry was the Credit Agreements Act.

This legislation never applied to money lending transactions, but applied to leasing, instalment sale agreements and credit transactions.

The Act introduced new concepts into the credit market such as the cooling off period for regulated transactions.

It also prescribed a fair legal process in situations where the credit grantor had to repossess goods that had been bought on credit following a default in payment.

The promulgation of the National Credit Act has been generally well received and it provided hope for the regulation of the industry.

CHAPTER 44

*"Life is like a hand of cards. You have to
play the hand you're dealt, you can't win by folding,
and sometimes you must take chances in order to win."*

– MIKE CONNER

WHAT IS DEBT COUNSELLING?

Trained individuals (called Debt Counsellors) will help you to deal with your debt. They will deal with your creditors and come to an agreement that allows you to cover your living expenses and apportion the remainder of your available funds to your creditors.

Debt Counsellors will conduct an independent enquiry into your financial circumstances and make recommendations to Credit Providers and the courts concerning restructuring your debt or even suspending "reckless" credit agreements.

You may not actually be "Over-Indebted" and qualify for "Debt Review"; in this case the Debt Counsellor will assist you to work out a better monthly budget which will enable you to repay your debts effectively.

The Debt Counsellor function is a Limited Statutory Function.

Debt Counsellors <u>should not give financial advice as dealt with in the Financial Advisory and Intermediary Services Act (Review of non-debt commitments).</u>

The function of a debt counsellor is a limited statutory function, whilst a debt counsellor is generally expected to assist the public in their financial matters they cannot act outside the parameters of their statutory function.

A debt counsellor cannot provide financial advice unless he is registered with the Financial Services Board as a financial advisor in terms of the Financial Advisory and Intermediary Services Act, 2002 9FAIS). Financial advice in terms of FAIS is defined as "…. any recommendation, guidance or proposal of a financial nature furnished, by any means or medium, to any client or group of clients" concerning:

- The purchase of financial products,

- Investments of any kind,

- Any loan linked to an investment or financial product,

- The termination, replacement, or variation of financial products.

The functions of a debt counsellor are detailed in terms of section 86. <u>They are limited to dealing with over-indebtedness and restructuring.</u>

The manner of dealing with these two issues is also limited in the Act.

This means that the duty of a debt counsellor is prescribed – he cannot just interfere in the affairs of the consumer. The decision of over-indebtedness or restructuring must be based on application by the consumer. Although it is not stated, it is not unlawful to consult with a consumer.

WHAT IS DEBT REVIEW?

This is the process of being assessed and assisted by a Debt Counsellor. The process begins with your application and ends with the issuing of a "Clearance Certificate" once all your debts are settled. The process time can vary, depending on how much debt you have to repay or by you (the consumer) failing to make you're agreed upon repayment.

WHAT DOES IT MEAN TO BE "OVER-INDEBTED"?

While this is now a legal term it basically means that anyone who, after deducting living expenses from their net salary, has less cash left over than the instalments on their total debt, may apply for counselling as they are probably "over-indebted".

WHAT ARE THE PRO'S AND CON'S OF DEBT COUNSELLING?

Pros:

- Once a consumer has made application for Debt review, Credit Providers can no longer attach any assets or take any further legal action against the consumer pending a determination by a Debt Counsellor as to whether the consumer is actually "Over-Indebted" or not. Should the consumer be "Over-Indebted" the consumer continues under Debt Review until all debt is settled.

- There is no permanent record of being under Debt Review kept on any Consumer Credit Bureau Data Base, meaning that unlike Administration or other avenues, the process leaves no black mark against your name.

- Repayment of your debt obligations is done through one regular monthly payment (to a Payment Distribution Agency who handles the money side of things).

- The Debt Counsellor will set aside a certain amount of income for your necessities (food, school fees, transport costs etc) and you then use whatever money you have left over to pay your debts. You will never pay more money than you can reasonably afford.

- A registered Debt Counsellor is far more likely to get a positive response from your creditors when it comes to negotiating your repayments than you might as a consumer.

- While under "debt review", you only make one monthly payment - to a Payment Distribution Agency - that in turn pays all your creditors. This one easy payment will make your finances much easier to manage and reduce your banking fees.

- A qualified Debt Counsellor will be able to advise you on ways to cut your monthly costs.

- Relief from all the stress of being in debt. You will get good advice and know that you are doing something about the problem. Knowing that one day the debt will gone, as will any record of it puts your mind at ease. No more letters you are too scared to open. No more phone calls you are too nervous to answer. Dealing with the problem rather than ignoring it gives you an instant feeling of relief.

Cons:

- While under debt review a person can no longer get access to new credit (which you don't want and cannot access anyway).

- While this may seem to be a negative thing, it is actually built into the process to protect consumers from becoming further indebted and to protect Credit Providers from being accused of "reckless lending".

DEBT COUNSELLORS ASSOCIATION OF SOUTH AFRICA

WHO IS DCASA?

DCASA is a voluntary association and professional body representing registered Debt Counsellors in South Africa.

It was established in 2007 with the commencement of the National Credit Act.

DCASA has contributed significantly to the industry by engaging with industry stakeholders to improve Debt Review. It is DCASA's aim to develop a streamlined Debt Counselling industry by setting process guidelines and training members with various products and services that will allow them to effectively and professionally deliver Debt Review service for over-indebtedness consumers.

The Association insists on a high and ethical behaviour on the part of their members to preserve and maintain the integrity and status of DCASA.

www.dcasa.co.za

CHAPTER 45

"Tough times never last, but tough people do."

– LYDIA SWEATT

POPI ACT – PROTECTION OF PERSONAL INFORMATION ACT, 2013

Information security law is an area of Law that asks whether you are protecting your information sufficiently. If a data breach happens, the relevant authority want to know steps you took to comply with information law.

What is the most valuable asset in your organisation? Perhaps you feel it is your staff or your equipment. But, for more and more organisations – information is their most valuable asset.

We do business in an information economy and you hold precious information in the forms of business records, customer data bases, and intellectual property.

You hire security personnel, install CCTV cameras, and have policies to protect your staff and equipment, but are you doing enough to protect your information?

WHAT DOES POPI STAND FOR?

THE PROTECTION OF PERSONAL INFORMATION.

POPI ACT

In simple terms, the purpose of the POPI ACT is to ensure that all South African institutions conduct themselves in a responsible manner when collecting, processing, storing and sharing another entity's personal information by holding them accountable should they abuse or compromise your personal information in any way.

The POPI legislation basically considers your personal information to be "precious goods" and therefore aims to bestow upon you, as the owner of your personal information certain rights of protection.

It must be noted that some personal information, on its own, does not necessarily allow a third party to confirm or infer someone's identity to the extent that this information can be used or abused for other purposes.

The combination of someone's name and phone number and/or email address for example is a lot more significant than just a name or phone number on its own.

As such the ACT defines a "unique identifier" to be data that "uniquely identifies that data subject in relation to that responsible party."

We have to accept that we now live in an information age and along with this progress comes the responsibility for each person to take care of and protect their own information.

Do not accuse someone else of sharing or compromising your personal information when you publish the very same information on public services like Facebook or LinkedIn.

Modern technology makes it very easy to access, collect and process high volumes of data at high speeds.

This information can then be sold, used for further processing and/or applied towards other ends.

In the wrong hands such ability can cause irreparable harm to individuals and companies.

It is important to note that this right to protection of "personal information" is not just applicable to a natural person (i.e. an individual) but <u>any legal entity,</u> including companies and also communities or other legally recognised organisations.

All of these entities are considered to be "data subjects" and afforded the same right to protection of their information.

As a company this would include protecting information about employees, vendors, service providers, business partners etc.

If you are a custodian of personal information it is important that you understand that there are serious implications for non-compliance.

The POPI ACT lists the following eight "conditions for the lawful processing of personal information, each containing their own sections.

- Accountability – Up to R10 million Rand in fines or 10 years in prison

- Processing Limitation

- Purpose Specification

- Further Processing Limitation

- Information Quality

- Openness (transparency)

- Security Safeguards

- Data Subject Participation

Implementing of POPI in your business does not have to be an onerous or even difficult a difficult task if you have implemented a <u>business nervous system</u> in your business.

The POPI legislation should be embraced and implemented in the spirit it was intended as its goal is to bring about a positive change and much needed protection for all.

Furthermore, implementing POPI creates an opportunity to simplify, review and streamline your business operations, policies and processes based on sound business practices and to embrace appropriate and cost effective technological solutions.

THE BUSINESS NERVOUS SYSTEM PHILOSPHY

"An organisation – including its resources, information and communication – in its entirety is a single body like any other organism found in nature, and therefore subject to the same rules as any other natural organism."

PROTECTION OF PERSONAL INFORMATION ACT, 2013, ACT NO 4 OF 2013

ACT

To promote the protection of personal information processed by public and private bodies; to introduce certain conditions so as to establish minimum requirements for the processing of personal information; to provide for the establishment of an Information Regulator to exercise certain powers and to perform certain duties and functions in terms of this ACT and the promotion of access to for the issuing of codes of conduct, INFORMATION ACT, 2000; to provide for the rights of persons regarding unsolicited electronic communications and automated decision making; to regulate the flow of personal information across the borders of the Republic; and to provide for matters connected therewith.

(www.justice.gov.za)

CHAPTER 46

"Life is not always perfect. Like a road, it has many bends, ups and downs, but that's its beauty."

– AMIT RAY

CRIMINAL LAW

Once again criminal law is an area that needs to be explored with a criminal lawyer.

I have seen several attorneys who don't specialize in criminal law and do the client a huge injustice.

Criminal law needs an attorney who can assist somebody no matter what the circumstances are.

Please, should you be asked to assist a friend, family member or anybody else with a criminal matter hand it over immediately to a qualified practising criminal lawyer.

PROPERTY LAW

Conveyancing or any other matter relating to property law takes somebody who is contract minded.

Many hours are spent perusing contracts, property sales and disagreements.

Again we are looking at somebody that is articulate in numbers, paper work and contracts.

This area of law is wide and the knowledge required takes years to fully comprehend.

I have met paralegals who absolutely excel at property law and are in high demand by law firms.

But, again don't receive the numeration that goes with the responsibilities.

One mistake can cost thousands if not hundreds of thousands of Rands.

BUSINESS LAW

In my opinion this area of law is endless and extremely exciting.

I believe that business law allows more scope to the paralegal than any other.

The opportunities are endless with so many new businesses starting up that need advice, the government setting aside millions to assist in start up businesses.

You will be blown away by the number of entrepreneurs that have the most incredible idea's but have no clue as to how to set up a business or the laws that surround the different business entities and tax laws.

If this is your area of interest get studying further, as there is a great need for knowledge to be of service.

LABOUR LAW

In my opinion this category goes hand in hand with business law.

Many practitioners would disagree with me I'm sure. If you are in the business law field, labour law comes with the territory and that is why I say they go together and this again leads to my comment that business law is exciting with many opportunities.

CHAPTER 47

"All dreams, hopes and wishes that you think about were given to you by a Higher Power that knows you absolutely have the ability to fulfil any or all of them."

– PETE ZAFRA

BECOMING A LEGAL STRATEGIST

I am sure many of my readers have seen the show 'Dr Bull' on TV. If not, I would really recommend that you do as it will give you a very good picture of what a legal strategist can offer clients and companies.

It is also one of the most exciting areas of law for me personally.

It really takes away the boredom of doing the same thing over and over on a daily basis.

Becoming a legal strategist goes hand in hand with companies outsourcing.

A legal strategist is a person often referred to as a chief legal strategist and should be empowered and provided with the support and resources necessary to champion high-level strategic efforts within the organization.

In a small or medium sized company, this person could be the legal officer or the general counsel.

As a legal consultant to clients and small businesses a paralegal can undertake compliance issues and other regulatory developments affecting plans and programs, providing advice on strategy and design.

WORKING WITH CLIENTS TO FORMULATE APPROACHES TO OPERATIONAL COMPLIANCE

In today's business world a legal consultant aren't just handling legal matters such as contracts, regulation, and litigation.

They are now balancing the concerns of both the business and of the law.

That makes the legal consultant both protector and enabler of the company's value.

Legal consultants also ensure the legal security of a company.

The in-house paralegal is involved in all phases of a project, preventing risks of litigation, and reviews litigation files.

He/she steers, leads, and co-ordinates in-house management, and plays a key role in negotiations and managing costs.

With the current changes in the business world, including the globalization sourcing/outsourcing of services, accessibility of "legal knowledge" on the internet, the growing demand for saving costs and providing "professional legal advice" in many areas of the law without spending resources and time on outside counsel.

As in-house legal consultants become a real business partners in the company, more and more legal departments (and even law schools) are focusing on training paralegals in areas beyond traditional law, such as business, finance, process and program management.

Legal departments are also beginning to focus on efficiency, productivity and cost saving, and at the same time – still protecting and defending the company from risk and liability.

With the growing demand of legal operations, professionals and expectations relating to their knowledge and skills, the face of the legal operations professions is also changing.

The "new legal operations professional" should not only understand the traditional issues, such as processes, cost-saving and internal communications – but also have a deep knowledge in the emerging legal technology (LegalTech) and have a deep understanding of the "legal aspects, risks and profession."

The demand for knowledge management is evolving and growing.

The legal consultant is no longer the only person who understands the "legal language" and the "potential risks" in a specific issue but rather the entire management team would like to understand such issues and to be able to make the right decisions.

In addition, there is a growing demand to "measure" the legal department like any other business unit and to make sure that it is a true business partner.

As anyone can see, there is a constant demand to deal with all the "non-legal" issues.

In a nutshell, legal operations is the set of business processes, activities and experts that optimize the delivery of legal services to an organization and maximises an in-house legal team's ability to protect and grow the company.

Each solution is customized and will vary depending on the size of the company and legal team, their strategy and needs.

Credit: (Adv. Edo Bar-Gil) www.lawflex.com

"There is real magic in enthusiasm. It spells the difference between mediocrity and accomplishment."

– VINCENT PEAL

KEEP UPDATED ON CASE STUDIES

I will for purposes of not boring you the reader I will keep this chapter very short!

If you are not serious about law and don't keep updated on the very many case studies then DO NOT BECOME A PARALEGAL SERVICE PROVIDER!

Law is an ongoing learning curve! Every day presents a new case or changes in our legal system.

Our new democracy is a vibrant ball of energy and changes take place daily. Keep up or get out!

"It doesn't matter where you came from. All that matters is where you are going."

– BRIAN TRACY

FIND YOUR FIRE

"Always bear in mind that your own resolution to success is more important than any other one thing."

– ABRAHAM LINCOLN

In this chapter I am hoping to assist you in 'finding your fire' as the entrepreneurial world can be a very lonely life, so hopefully, you will find some quotes and stories that will inspire you to do your best.

I have taken the liberty of sharing a couple of points that I believe will carry you through the difficult times and the positive times.

1. **Set a personal mission statement**

   Every entrepreneur should have a vision statement. It should serve as a constant reminder about your purpose of becoming an entrepreneur.

2. **Make a plan**

   The purpose here is to have a clear understanding of what you want to accomplish personally and how you will achieve it.

3. **Start with a routine**

Getting yourself motivated is about getting started.

For this reason, you should start every day with a great morning routine, which will help your mind and body to be alert, focused and prepared to create new habits.

As part of your routine every morning, you should spend time reviewing and refining your plan.

4. **Set time for yourself**

Because entrepreneurs can often get completely caught up in their business, it is important to set personal time during the day for yourself.

During this time, allow yourself the flexibility to take a walk, think and meditate or even exercise.

5. **Plan ahead and set reminders**

Develop a habit of setting reminders throughout the day for the important tasks and daily goals you have set.

6. **Set rewards**

We are naturally wired to react to incentives, so be prepared to reward yourself for accomplishing a goal or maintaining a habit.

Just like in business, you should recognize and reward small victories along the way to long-term, broader goals.

7. **Engage friends**

Sometimes the best motivation comes from peer pressure.

Engage your friends and colleagues to help motivate you towards individual and shared goals.

8. **Indulge in inspirational activities**

Sometimes, you just need to look outside your circle for motivation.

9. **Stay positive**

There is no one-size-fits all answer to what makes people happy.

Choose the phrase "I'm happy."

By saying that phrase and mustering up an authentic smile, I find my mood and motivation is automatically elevated.

10. **Sleep**

Finally, never underestimate the value of a good night sleep for personal motivation.

I have found that, with a few exceptions, no unfinished task or missed goal is worth the misery that comes with loss of sleep.

More important, with a fresh night of rest, these tasks and goals become infinitely easier to accomplish the following day.

(Credit: Peter Gasca) www.entrepeneur.com

I further add to this chapter with the following suggestions:

RELIVE PAST SUCCESSES

Do you remember what it felt like to reach an accomplishment?

Spend time thinking about the process you went through, the work you put in and the taste of victory.

Reliving some of your best moments can get you over the hurdle and into action.

FIND INSPIRATION IN SOMEONE ELSE

There will always be others who have walked the path before you, faced challenges and emerged victorious.

Spend time appreciating the drive and determination of others, and explore how they overcame challenges they faced on their journeys.

This can be motivating, while also giving you some creative ideas for getting through challenges you're facing.

TRY A NEW APPROACH

Progress often generates routines; routines can bring boredom; and boredom can cause a loss of motivation.

IF YOUR ROUTINES ARE CAUSING YOU TO LOSE YOUR FIRE, IT MAY BE TIME TO SHAKE THINGS UP.

Start to question your standard processes, and introduce a new way of thinking to get past complacency and renew your motivation.

Starting, growing and running a business can be a thankless and exhausting process, but it can also be very rewarding in many ways even if you don't make it rich overnight.

So when the money is not (yet) pouring in, will you get discouraged or keep pressing forward?

If you are passionate about more than simply making money, you are more likely to be willing to continue making necessary sacrifices until the big income starts rolling in.

If your motivation is to start a paralegal service and it is something you are passionate about, you are likely to suffer from fewer emotional setbacks and entrepreneur burnout when you find out it takes time to build independent wealth.

You will be more patient with yourself and your business as it grows, and you will make better business decisions.

Business owners that are exclusively motivated by money often have unreasonable expectations of getting rich quick.

When financial goals are your only important goals, you will miss out on the many other rewards of being self-employed including a sense of accomplishment, purpose, and the rewards of knowing who you are and doing something worthwhile with your life.

(Credit: Lahle Wolfe; 2019)

"Remember that wherever your heart is, there you will find your treasure."

– PAULO COELHO (THE ALCHEMIST, PG 111)

"Foxes are people who embrace uncertainty and believe that experience – doing things – is an essential source of knowledge. Action sorts out the sheep from the goats!"

– CHANTELL ILBURY AND CLEM SUNTER

(THE MIND OF THE FOX; PG 11)

IN CLOSING

*"There are as many unhappy rich people as
there are unhappy poor people."*

— JOHAN CLAASSENS

As I have written this book I have come to realise the need for paralegals in South Africa. As we now know, how Legal Aid South Africa works and how attorneys work I have come to believe that the legal system works for those who have and those who have not which leaves me thinking of the people in the middle of our society. The middle class! These people don't qualify for Legal Aid South Africa but also can't afford the exorbitant fees of our legal system. So, where do they go for solid assistance? Paralegals of course! As the world's economy goes into a decline the more middle class people are going to struggle to make ends meet. As a paralegal you can fit into the middle class market by assisting these people. Many clients are prepared to be assisted by good paralegals to a point where the file must be handed over to an attorney. A paralegal worth his/her salt will be able to mediate most cases successfully so the hours spent at court will be kept to a minimum for the client. Always remember that you are not an attorney so do not act as one. A paralegal is a person who assists clients with paperwork and setting them in the right direction for further legal advice. Do not compromise your position. Be a mediator and leave the fighting to the attorneys.

I truly wish that one day our legal system will see the benefit that paralegals can offer to our country and all who live in it. Maybe, one day we will be recognised as an integral spoke in the wheel of law that seems to turn very slowly. The courts are backing up with matters and cases that can be easily settled before expensive litigation takes place, if only the system would allow it to happen. Paralegals should be seen as mediators and attorneys as the fighters.

Here, I refer to a case namely *"Brownlee v Brownlee."*

Lawyers are obliged to recommend mediation, as a result of which attorney's could be deprived of their costs, along with parties who unreasonably refuse to mediate.

These are among the conclusions drawn by John Brand, alternate dispute resolution specialist at Commercial law firm Bowman and Gilfillan, in the wake of the South Gauteng High Court ruling in Brownlee v Brownlee.

> "The court held that the failure by attorneys to send a matter to mediation at an early stage should be visited by the courts displeasure," says Brand. "The court limited the costs that the attorneys could recover from their clients to those that they could tax on the party and party scale and thereby deprived them of their full attorney and client fees."

I would recommend that all readers should research this case as there is important information for the paralegal/mediator. Mr Brand ends his article by saying "Mediation will in time become an integral part of our civil justice system."

With that in mind, I ask that you the reader to please keep your eyes peeled for my next book "Psychology of Mediation and Human Behaviour."

I hope that by now you as a paralegal would have realized that there are many area's open for you to assist in, and that the paralegal role in South Africa is vast and exciting.

My last recommendation to all paralegals is to study further and add to your paralegal diploma.

Paralegal + Mediator Certification = Success

Paralegal + Debt Counselling Certification = Success

Paralegal + Psychology Counselling Certificate = Success

Paralegal + Legal Strategy = Success

Now combine all of the above into one package and you will be the most sought after paralegal in the industry. You will have more work than many attorneys.

Remember that many companies are outsourcing and the market is growing by the day.

I thank all the paralegals/mediators who have invested their hard earned money in my book and my greatest wish is that this handbook will assist you in earning a great deal more because of its contents.

I can be contacted via email or Facebook (Dr Johan Claassens – Author) or www.johanclaassens.com for dates and further information on my workshops around the country.

Be Daring – Be Different

"Let us be bold. Let us be brave. Let us be together."

– BRAD HENRY